Baby Signing
FOR
DUMMIES

by Jennifer Watson

WILEY

Wiley Publishing, Inc.

Baby Signing For Dummies®

Published by
Wiley Publishing, Inc.
111 River St.
Hoboken, NJ 07030-5774
www.wiley.com

Copyright © 2006 by Wiley Publishing, Inc., Indianapolis, Indiana

Published simultaneously in Canada

For general information on our other products and services, please contact our Customer Care Department within the U.S. at 800-762-2974, outside the U.S. at 317-572-3993, or fax 317-572-4002.

For technical support, please visit www.wiley.com/techsupport.

Wiley also publishes its books in a variety of electronic formats. Some content that appears in print may not be available in electronic books.

Library of Congress Control Number: 2006927728

ISBN-13: 978-0-471-77386-3

ISBN-10: 0-471-77386-7

Manufactured in the United States of America

10 9 8 7 6 5 4 3 2 1

1B/RS/QZ/QW/IN

WILEY

About the Author

Jennifer Hill Watson is the mom to three signing children. She began signing with her first daughter when her daughter was about 6 months old. At 4½ years, her oldest now has over 300 signs. Jennifer's second daughter is nearing 300 signs at age 3½. Her son has 116 signs and 154 words at 19 months.

A former teacher, Jennifer has taught in both private schools and Houston public schools. She teaches signing classes for babies and their parents in the Houston area and helps lead the Houston Signing Babies support group both on the Web and at regular meetings. Jennifer also speaks at national conferences to teachers on using American Sign Language in the classroom.

Jennifer works with McGraw-Hill/Wright Group's Early Childhood Division as an Early Childhood Consultant and teacher trainer. She volunteers as director of a preschool choir and leads confirmation classes with sixth graders in her church.

She has a bachelor of science from Texas Wesleyan University in Fort Worth, Texas. Jennifer and her family currently live in Katy, Texas.

Dedication

For my very own signing babies, Darby Grace, Aidan Elizabeth, and Cole Thomas. And for my wonderful husband, Billy — their amazing signing daddy.

Author's Acknowledgments

What a joy to acknowledge just some of the people who helped make this book possible. I feel like I've just birthed my fourth baby, taking five months of hard labor to push this book out. You don't do that kind of work all alone.

First and foremost, a *huge* thank-you to Beryt Nisenson, who got this ball rolling in the first place. Beryt helped me get started teaching classes and then gave me the contact to potentially write this book — and it worked out. Additionally, she provided limitless support and love before and during the writing of this book — as I'm sure she will after this book is finished. You're an amazing inspiration in so many ways. I'm so grateful you're my friend. Thank you.

Another thank-you goes out to Jessica Faust, my agent and communicator throughout the entire writing of this book. Thanks for finding the Web site and contacting us, as well as supporting me directly throughout.

Generous appreciation goes out to Sandy Blackthorn who held my hand while I organized my thoughts, let go as needed, and then turned my thoughts and words into *For Dummies* thoughts and words. You're a great teacher, Sandy! More appreciation goes out to my project editor, Elizabeth Kuball, who coordinated it all (wow!); my acquisitions editor, Tracy Boggier, who has supported and directed throughout; my technical editor, Nancy Mitchum, who helped keep the ASL as "pure" as it could possibly be in this setting; and my illustrator, Lisa Reed. Your support and guidance have been invaluable throughout this project. Thank you.

About halfway into this project, I took a fall, broke my left wrist, and had a cast on until after the book's completion (roughly three months). Needless to say, that made typing just a bit difficult. Thank you to my typists (you know who you are) for being my "fingers," and sometimes my brain, until the end of the typing. And thank you to all the editors for all your patience, understanding, and support through the broken-wrist fiasco. Thank you to Doni for providing my family with meals every week and giving my family the chance to eat healthy as I wrote the last quarter of this book. What an amazing friend.

Karen H., thanks for the coffee breaks. I'm going to miss you.

Thank you, thank you, thank you to Heather for supporting me with phone calls, e-mails and prayers from start to finish. Without you, this book may not be here. Love you, girl.

And to those of you in Mother's Share Group, in Generation Acts, in the office, at church, and beyond who encouraged me with a quick smile or word as I attempted to put one foot in front of the other in the writing of this book, thank you. A special thank-you to those of you in these same groups who took me "out" in various and sundry ways when I needed a break.

Thanks to all the grandparents (DeeDee, Grandpa Tom, Pampu, GranJan, GranT, Pachie-Achie, Pawpaw, and my Memaw) for loving and supporting me throughout the life of this project. From babysitting at times to gift certificates and general support, you've all been incredible. Thank you.

Without my three signing babies — Darby, Aidan Elizabeth, and Cole — baby signing might not even be on my radar. Your daddy and I began signing with you as young infants and you continue to inspire me and keep me signing with babies, toddlers, their parents, and beyond. You are such a gift. Thank you.

And to my husband Billy, thank you for putting up with the ups and downs and ins and outs of my relationship with this book. It's not easy to put up with the idiosyncrasies of late hours mixed with double-duty childcare. What a gift you are. I'm grateful for you every day. Thank you. I love you.

Publisher's Acknowledgments

We're proud of this book; please send us your comments through our Dummies online registration form located at www.dummies.com/register/.

Some of the people who helped bring this book to market include the following:

Acquisitions, Editorial, and Media Development

Project Editor: Elizabeth Kuball

Acquisitions Editor: Tracy Boggier

Editorial Program Coordinator: Hanna K. Scott

Technical Editor: Nancy Mitchum

Consultant: Sandy Blackthorn

Editorial Manager: Michelle Hacker

Editorial Supervisor and Reprint Editor: Carmen Krikorian

Editorial Assistant: Erin Calligan, David Lutton

Cartoons: Rich Tennant (www.the5thwave.com)

Composition Services

Project Coordinator: Patrick Redmond

Layout and Graphics: Carl Byers, Joyce Haughey, Stephanie D. Jumper, Heather Ryan

Illustrator: Lisa Reed

Proofreaders: Leeann Harney, Christy Pingleton, Techbooks

Indexer: Techbooks

Publishing and Editorial for Consumer Dummies

> **Diane Graves Steele,** Vice President and Publisher, Consumer Dummies
>
> **Joyce Pepple,** Acquisitions Director, Consumer Dummies
>
> **Kristin A. Cocks,** Product Development Director, Consumer Dummies
>
> **Michael Spring,** Vice President and Publisher, Travel
>
> **Kelly Regan,** Editorial Director, Travel

Publishing for Technology Dummies

> **Andy Cummings,** Vice President and Publisher, Dummies Technology/General User

Composition Services

> **Gerry Fahey,** Vice President of Production Services
>
> **Debbie Stailey,** Director of Composition Services

Contents at a Glance

Table of Contents

Part II: Ready, Set, Sign! 35

Chapter 4: Signing 101: Some Basic Signs..........37

Chapter 5: Eat, Baby, Eat! Mealtime Signs..........51

Introduction

● ●

*P*lain and simple, *Baby Signing For Dummies* is about connecting with your hearing baby or toddler. It's about building a bridge between you and what's going on in your child's mind: what she wants, what she needs, what she thinks, and how she feels. Now, I'm not saying you'll be able to read her mind. But you *will* be able to understand some of the things on her mind before she's able to express them with spoken words. This book enables you and your baby to use American Sign Language (ASL) to communicate long before your baby can speak.

This ability to communicate through sign language reduces tantrums, which babies throw because they know what they want and expect you to know, too. In addition, it reduces the frustrations that parents feel from frantically attempting to interpret babies' unintelligible grunts and screams. And it increases meaningful parent-child interactions, which opens the door to untold benefits for both you and your baby.

I know of what I speak. I have three signing children (and a signing husband), who have all signed since they were seven months old or younger (well, not the husband). I began this signing journey when my oldest was 4 weeks old. A book on a relative's coffee table piqued my interest. I held the idea in the back of my mind for a few weeks as I continued to adjust to my new identity as a mother. Then one day I saw the book again while browsing at my local bookstore. Though I had my doubts, I figured it couldn't hurt to buy the book and check it out. So I did.

My oldest is now 4 years old and has a signing vocabulary of over 300 signs. So, as you can see, it works! The experience of signing with my children has changed me from a skeptical new mom buying yet another parenting book into a teacher who helps other parents get to know how to sign with their babies and into the author of the book you hold in your hands. The reason I wrote this book is to share with you my passion for signing with babies and to make your entry into the world of signing with your baby as easy and as joyful as possible.

About This Book

The shelves of bookstores are brimming these days with books about signing with your baby. This book is different for many reasons. First off, it's different because it was written from within the trenches. I have three preschoolers at home. I've learned a lot in the four years I've been signing with my babies. Some of what I've learned has been very helpful; some of it not so much. I plan on sharing the former with you, saving you from repeating my mistakes and from wasting your valuable time.

Also, I know you don't want to be an expert in the field of signing with babies. I mean, who has time for that? You do, after all, have a baby. And you just want to be able to communicate with him as soon as possible. I hear ya and know first hand where you're coming from. To this day, all I want to do is enhance communication with my children and help other parents do the same in the easiest and most rewarding way possible.

This book is all about easy and rewarding. The information is laid out in reference form so you can easily find exactly what you're looking for without having to read the book from front to back in chronological order. The instructions are straightforward. The illustrations are easy to follow. The stories are all true and draw on personal experiences. You'll laugh. You'll cry. You'll feel like this book was written just for you by someone who knows exactly what you're going through — because it was.

Conventions Used in This Book

A few conventions are used throughout this book:

- CAPITAL letters are used to indicate ASL signs in the text. For example, the sign for BATH is covered in Chapter 7.

- *Italic* type is used to highlight words that are being defined, as well as to emphasize certain words or points. For example, *American Sign Language* is the official name of the official sign language for the deaf. It's often referred to as *ASL*. And I'm here to tell you that even before babies can control the movements necessary to produce speech, they *can* control the movements necessary to produce some ASL signs.

- **Boldface** type is used to indicate the action part of numbered steps, such as physically moving your hand into a certain position. For example, to sign BATH, follow these steps:

1. **With both hands, make loose fists, thumbs on top.**

2. **Place your fists on your chest like you're Tarzan getting ready to beat on your chest.**

3. **Move your fists in several circles as if scrubbing your chest.**

✔ `Monofont` type is used to indicate Web addresses and e-mail addresses. When this book was printed, some Web addresses may have needed to break across two lines of text. If that happened, rest assured that we haven't put in any extra characters (such as hyphens) to indicate the break. So, when using one of these Web addresses, just type in exactly what you see in this book, pretending as though the line break doesn't exist.

Something else I should point out is that I've made every effort to alternate male and female pronouns when referring to babies throughout this book. I have two girls and a boy, and I love them all equally. I didn't get out the calculator and tally up the pronouns (who has time for that?!), so if there are more of one gender than another, rest assured that baby signing works equally well with boys and with girls — my three kids are a testament to that!

What You're Not to Read

Technically speaking, because this is a reference book and not a classroom academic text, you can pick and choose what you are and aren't going to read. I hope, of course, that you'll want to read each and every word. However, know that some material in here is truly skippable. By that, I mean certain material isn't essential for you to know in order to successfully sign with your baby. The material is still valuable — but in a bonus, supplementary way. Here's what you can safely skip:

✔ **The sidebars:** You'll see shaded boxes here and there throughout the book. They're sidebars, and they contain side stories and personal accounts that complement a topic discussed in the book.

✔ **The appendixes:** Tucked neatly into the back of this book are three appendixes, covering the ASL alphabet, the numbers one through ten, and some colors. Knowing these signs isn't absolutely essential to signing with babies, but many people ask me about them anyway. I've included them in this book in case you're interested, too.

Foolish Assumptions

You know the old adage that assumptions can be dangerous. So I want to be upfront with you and share a few assumptions I made about the reader (that would be you) as I wrote this book:

- ✓ **You have a baby or toddler in your life with whom you'd like to communicate.** This book was written for parents and caregivers like yourself (and like me), whether it's your first time in the ring or whether caring for a baby or toddler is old hat to you.

- ✓ **You've already heard something about signing with babies that sparked your interest and led you to this book.** You may have seen it in a movie or have friends who use it with their family. Perhaps you saw an article in a parenting magazine or a newspaper. Like me, you may simply have been intrigued when you saw a book about signing with your baby online or at your local bookstore. This book was written to fan into a flame that spark of interest.

- ✓ **You are at least a tad skeptical.** Maybe you're concerned about the amount of time you'll have to invest in this whole signing-with-baby experience. You're worried how fluent you'll have to become in American Sign Language. You're not sure signing with babies even works. Maybe it's just a gimmick or the latest parenting fad. I've faced those doubts and questions myself and helped countless other parents address them. This book answers the skeptic's questions because it's written by a former skeptic.

- ✓ **Most of all, you love your baby.** You want what's best for him and hope to give him every advantage you can in life. You need to know what's going on in that precious little mind as you see those wheels spinning. And you're anxious to open the lines of communication with him as soon as possible. This book will help you do this.

How This Book Is Organized

When using a reference book, it's always helpful to know where to find things. So to help you find things in this book, I've divided it into six parts, each of which contains chapters related to the theme of that part. Here's a brief description to help you navigate.

Part 1: Talking Hands

This part provides you with a basic overview of signing with babies. Here, you find out why you should use sign language to communicate with your baby. You also find the basic building blocks to help you set out on this great adventure.

Part 11: Ready, Set, Sign!

Eating, sleeping, getting clean . . . these are all part of your little one's daily routine (and yours). In this part, you discover how to incorporate signing into these bare necessities of life. You also find out how signing can assist you in your number-one priority: keeping baby safe and sound.

Part 111: Signs for Everyday Life

Babies love to play and have fun. They're fascinated with the world around them. Here, you find out how to use baby's sense of wonder to open all kinds of doors of signing opportunity.

Part 1V: Now We're Talking

After your baby is an established signer, use this part to take signing to the next level. String multiple signs together for a signed "sentence" to communicate more fully. Iron out the rough patches you're bound to face along the way, and find out how signing can be a big part of your family's long-term future.

Part V: The Part of Tens

Here, you find ten reasons to sign with your baby, ten signs every baby and toddler should know, ten songs to sign along with, and ten resources to enhance your signing journey.

Appendixes

Here, you can discover the signs for letters, numbers, and colors to aid you on your way.

Icons Used in This Book

Scattered throughout this book you'll find icons in the margins. They highlight certain kinds of information that you may find beneficial.

This icon indicates helpful pointers or bits of advice for signing with baby. These tips are based on my experience and that of other signing families. They may help you avoid some pitfalls along the way.

This icon points out important information that you'll want to keep in mind during your signing journey.

Tied to this icon you'll find success stories from my family as well as other baby-signing families. These can be a great source of encouragement while waiting to have a few success stories of your own. I can't wait to hear yours! You're welcome to contact me through my Web site at www.imaginationsigners.com.

Where to Go from Here

Unlike most books, this one wasn't written to be read straight through from cover to cover. Feel free to skip around if you find a particular chapter or heading that interests you. If you're looking for a good place to start other than Chapter 1, I suggest Chapter 14, which provides ten reasons to sign with your baby. Chapter 3 is also a great place to begin, especially the do's and don'ts section. Or just look over the table of contents and see what interests you. Wherever you choose to start, happy signing to you and your baby!

Part I
Talking Hands

In this part . . .

Can hands talk? You bet they can, and I'm not just referring to the "talking" they may do when someone cuts you off in traffic. Hands can also talk through American Sign Language (ASL), a beautiful and expressive language used by people of all ages with hearing impairments of varying degrees. The neat thing is, about 30 years ago someone stumbled onto the realization that hearing babies can use sign language to communicate, too — *way* before they can actually speak. It took a while for the general public to catch on, but in recent years, the popularity of baby signing has skyrocketed.

In Part I of this book, you discover what baby signing is all about, some of the research behind it, and why you should do it with your baby. You also get tips on how to introduce sign language to your baby and even take a trip to boot camp for some basic training. Off you go — have a grand time!

Chapter 1

Getting Onboard with Baby Signing

In This Chapter
▶ Answering frequently asked questions about baby signing
▶ Trying your first sign — so you can rest assured that you *can* do this

*I*n the course of a typical week, I get tons of questions about signing with babies. The questions come from inquiring minds in settings such as play groups, meetings, grocery stores, phone calls from friends, and, of course the classes I teach on the subject. Even people who don't have children in the baby or toddler stage are typically fascinated with the subject. Imagine . . . a window into a baby or young child's mind before he can speak. What a gift to both parents and children!

In this chapter, I go over some of the most common questions I encounter on signing with babies. Use this chapter as an opportunity to get comfortable with the concept of baby sign language — to get onboard, so to speak — and then get ready to open the gift of signing with your own little sweetie pie.

What Exactly Is Sign Language for Babies?

I always enjoy hearing this question because it gives me a chance to rekindle the initial excitement I felt after asking the same question way back when. This question means someone is curious, and because she's asking me about signing with babies, it's my job to excite her about the subject just as someone once excited me — and subsequently changed my world.

Many people assume that babies don't speak because they don't understand. But the truth is, babies understand a great deal. Think about it: Only one thing satisfies a hungry baby, and that's a full tummy. And a hungry baby will scream and scream until you give him the means to fill his tummy. He can't say, "Hey, you! Feed me!" But that's exactly what he's thinking when he screams until you feed him.

The reason babies don't speak isn't for lack of understanding. It's for lack of the ability to control the movements of the mouth and tongue that are necessary to produce intelligible, audible speech. Those movements are undeveloped until babies are older. However, at a much earlier age, babies *can* control the movements necessary to produce signs. And as a result of this ability, a world of two-way communication can be opened for babies and their caregivers.

Which leads, of course, to the answer to the question "What exactly is sign language for babies?" Sign language for babies is a method of using either invented hand gestures or American Sign Language (ASL) to communicate with very young children months and even years before they can communicate verbally. (Note that American Sign Language is the official name of the official sign language for the deaf. Later in this chapter is a section called "Should I Use ASL or Make Up My Own Signs?" Take a gander at that section to get my take on that question.)

Why Should I Sign with My Baby?

Signing with babies provides many benefits. Consider these, for example:

- ✔ **Signing gives babies a voice by giving them a way to communicate their wants, needs, and observations.** Instead of simply trying to guess what a crying baby needs, for example, a parent or caregiver can understand the need because the baby signs MILK or BALL or FINISHED. Of course, this doesn't mean the crying stops altogether, but frustration levels are drastically reduced because — through the signs that the baby can make — he can communicate some of his specific wants, needs, and observations. (By the way, I cover the signs for MILK and FINISHED in Chapter 5, and I show you the sign for BALL in Chapter 10.)

- ✔ **According to research done by Baby Signs (www.babysigns. com), by the time children who signed as babies and toddlers are in second grade, their IQ scores are an average of 12 points higher than the IQ scores of their non-signing peers.** So, beyond the here-and-now benefits of giving babies a voice and reducing frustration levels, signing has long-term benefits as well. (See Chapter 13 for details about signing children and IQ scores, grades, and ADD/ADHD.)

✔ **Speech stimulates a particular part of a person's brain.** Children who have chatty, interactive parents typically have more stimulation in the speech center of their brains. That's pretty cool in and of itself, but now consider this: Children who are exposed to a secondary language have stimulation in an additional part of their brains as they're exposed to and learn the language. And here's the biggie for purposes of this book: According to research done by Dr. Marilyn Daniels, children who sign as part of their language development have stimulation in a third, *kinesthetic* (movement-based sensory experience) portion of their brains.

✔ **Signing a word makes that word more concrete because the child is not only hearing the word but also seeing the sign for the word, seeing the object of the sign, and feeling the movement of the sign.** Repeatedly experiencing the sign will eventually lead to a child's responding to the sign through obvious understanding or using the sign or word itself.

Speech delays and signing: They're not related

My second daughter, Aidan Elizabeth, was diagnosed with a speech delay at 22 months. Her doctor reluctantly wrote the referral for speech testing, telling me he was humoring me by doing so. The reason for his reluctance came from his belief that speech-delayed children showed a symptom of frustration because they couldn't communicate, and he knew from discussions with me that Aidan Elizabeth wasn't frustrated because she *could* communicate with her family — through signs. At the time, in fact, she knew around 125 signs. Aidan Elizabeth wasn't frustrated — because she had a means to communicate.

Now, her older sister, Darby, who was almost 3 years old at the time, knew around 175 signs and conversed with the maturity of a much older child. I mention this because it turns out that one of the potential reasons for Aidan Elizabeth's speech delay was having a talkative older sister. The theory was that Aidan Elizabeth didn't need to talk because Darby talked for her.

Aidan Elizabeth qualified for speech therapy and has made significant strides in her speech development, but here's the take-home point for you: She would've had the speech delay whether we signed with her or not. Signing didn't cause the speech delay. In contrast, I hate to think about how frustrating her life would've been *without* signs.

Even after I explain the benefits of signing with babies, some folks worry that signing might delay their babies' speech. Rest assured, research has repeatedly proven that signing children actually begin to speak earlier and speak more often than their non-signing counterparts. According to Dr. Michelle Anthony and Dr. Reyna Lindert's research into signing babies, by 18 months of age, an average Signing Smart child will have 94 signs and 105 spoken words. By stark contrast, a typical non-signing 18-month-old has 10 to 50 spoken words. (Signing Smart [`www.signingsmart.com`] is a signing program for hearing babies and toddlers that promotes ASL signs.)

Should I Use ASL or Make Up My Own Signs?

Know up front that either made-up signs or American Sign Language (ASL) will achieve the goal of communicating more easily with your baby until he can talk. In this book, though, I solely use ASL, so you know where I stand.

Think of it this way. Your child says "wah-wah" and you know and understand that he wants water. All of the experts tell you to signify your understanding but to continue to model the correct pronunciation. My reason for preferring ASL signs over invented gestures is the same. Besides, if I'm going to go to the trouble of figuring out and passing on an additional language to my child, I think I'll invest in a real language — ASL. I mean, sure, Pig Latin is fun and it communicates — but Latin it ain't.

Use ASL and open all kinds of doors

When my oldest daughter, Darby, was 11 months old (and I was seven months pregnant with her sister), we went out to eat at a local restaurant. In the process of the meal, Darby signed MORE. Right away we heard an excited exclamation from a hearing-impaired young man at the next table: "She signed MORE! She signed MORE!"

He immediately came over and began signing and speaking to us. We clarified that no one in our family was hearing impaired and we weren't fluent in conversational ASL, and then we shared with the young man our reasons for signing with our baby. He was not only fascinated with the concept but also grateful to us for showing our child how to communicate in his language.

By the way, you can find the sign for MORE, as well as other mealtime signs, in Chapter 5.

When Should I Start and When Will My Baby Start Signing Back?

In very general terms, it's never too early to start signing with your baby. Consider this: Do you wait until a baby can speak before you speak to him? Of course not. You introduce words from the very beginning — and you can do the same with signs.

That said, however, you have to be mindful of how many signs you introduce to your baby early on (see Chapter 2), and you *can't* expect a newborn to sign back. The younger you start signing to your baby, the longer it'll take for her to sign back. On the flipside, if you start signing when the baby is older, she'll probably respond more quickly.

Like many milestones in babies' lives, there's simply no hard-and-fast rule for knowing when your baby will start signing back. Each child is different and responds to signing in different ways. And each family is different and uses signing differently.

Turn to Chapter 2 for the nitty-gritty details on the right time to introduce signs to your baby, where and how to begin, when your baby might start signing back, and who else to bring onboard to sign with your baby.

Many families keep from signing with their babies because they think they're too late. I can't tell you how often I've heard, "Maybe we'll sign with the *next* baby." Maybe so. The truth is, it's never too late to start signing with your children. They'll benefit from the experience regardless of their age.

When Should I Stop?

The decision to stop signing is very much an individual decision. Know that continuing the journey past babyhood does provide long-term benefits (see Chapter 13). I still sign with Darby, my oldest, and she's 4 years old. She still signs back to me. In fact, she still asks me to show her *new* signs. She loves signing and finds it fun and useful. For example, there are times when Darby gets a little wound up and can't seem to find the right words to communicate. During those times, signing naturally takes over as she communicates through ASL instead of speech.

My whole family has terrific fun going about our lives and naturally adding signing into our routines. Signing keeps the kids distracted during a long wait at the doctor's office, for example, as we play "I Spy . . ." using color signs (see Appendix C). On rainy days when we're stuck inside, we sometimes learn new songs or read new stories, and we pick out a character or two to focus on and sign all the way through. (Check out Chapter 16 for some great signing songs and look in Chapter 7 for the sign for BOOK.) And I can even tell my kids to "STOP!" across a crowded room or at the local park by signing instead of screaming. (STOP and other safe-and-sound signs are located in Chapter 6. Signs related to the great outdoors, including the family park, are located in Chapter 10.)

In other words, signing shouldn't be a chore. It should be fun and not forced. That's the way it is in my family, and we have no plans to quit anytime soon.

What Should I Sign with My Baby?

Which words to sign is one of the most difficult decisions to make when you're just starting out signing with your baby. Because ASL is an actual language, literally thousands of signs exist. Just buy an ASL dictionary and you'll see what I mean. Choosing your repertoire can be overwhelming, but a few simple guidelines can help you decide which signs to use for your baby.

To begin, look around you. What is common to your world now that baby is here? Start by signing a couple of the things that are part of baby's everyday life. Things like MILK (including formula) and BATH are pretty consistent in baby's day-to-day experience, so those signs would probably work nicely. You probably also find yourself frequently asking baby if he wants to EAT or DRINK or is TIRED and ready for BED — all worthy signs, too.

There are likely also a few things that really get your baby excited, like maybe the family DOG or the FISH in the aquarium at the doctor's office. Or maybe your baby is inseparable from her teddy BEAR or BLANKET. Identify objects that your baby is really interested in (with my youngest, Cole, the fascinating object was a HAT for a while), and you'll start to build a useful and fun list of signs.

As you're getting started, use this book as your guide for some handy words to sign. Chapter 4, for example, focuses on some basic signs that may be perfect for your baby. Or look through Chapters 5 through 10, which provide signs in themed groups — signs specifically for meals, safety, bath, bed, clothing, animals, and the great outdoors. Or if you're a just-gimme-the-top-ten kind of person, turn to Chapter 15 for ten signs every baby or toddler should know. And when you're ready, Chapter 11 covers how to sign some simple word "sentences."

I'm Just Regular Folk — Can I Really Do This?

You may be overwhelmed by the thought of figuring out ASL, remembering all those signs, and becoming a signing coach to your baby. You're not alone. Many who start down the path of signing with their babies turn back because of worries over those very things.

In fact, my own husband was reluctant when we began signing with our first baby. He had studied Spanish in high school and college, and Greek in college and graduate school. The experience was enough to convince him that foreign languages are not his strong suit. The thought of tackling another language, especially one as unique as ASL, was a little scary for him.

But the point is not to learn an entire new language. You don't have to know all of ASL to sign with your baby. You only have to figure out and become proficient with the individual signs that are of value to you and your baby. And you only have to do so at a pace that keeps you one step ahead of your baby's learning curve. Even my reluctant husband manages to do this and do it well. Seriously, if you take the process a handful of signs at a time, you'll be amazed at how much you can remember. And you'll be blown away at how much, over time, your baby can remember, too.

As for the coaching part, some people seem to be born to teach. There are at least eight school teachers in my immediate family, and although I denied it for many years, I'm one of them. Maybe you're not born to teach, and that's okay. You can still coach your baby to communicate with sign language. In this book, I provide you with tools to help make the task easier. Chapter 3, for example, is kind of like a boot camp for getting in the right mindset and "handset" (so to speak) as you prepare to sign with your baby. It covers some basic hand shapes as well as some general do's and don'ts — tips and hints to help you along the way. In addition, because a few signs encompass individual letters of the ASL alphabet, I've included illustrations of the entire ASL alphabet in Appendix A. Plus, every sign covered in this book is accompanied by step-by-step directions and an illustration for making the sign. If you hit a stumbling block, check out Chapter 12 for some guidance. And if you're so inclined, check out Chapter 17 for info about some outside resources (Web sites, videos, and signing schools and courses) for additional help.

But right here and now, I want you to check out how easy signing can be. I want to show you how to make the sign for a very versatile word — WHAT. You can simultaneously say and sign this word in all sorts of conversations and situations. While you and baby are looking at a storybook together, for example, you can point to an object on a page and excitedly say and sign, "WHAT is that?!" Or if baby is crying, you can wipe away the tears while gently saying and signing, "WHAT is wrong?" Here you go:

1. **Place your elbows to your sides, hands extended, palms up.**

2. **Shake your hands a bit in the natural gesture for "What?" (see Figure 1-1).**

Figure 1-1: Say WHAT?

Chapter 2

Introducing Signs to Your Baby

So, you've decided to use sign language with your baby or toddler. Great. Now what? You may be feeling overwhelmed and don't know when, where, or how to start. Well, relax. This chapter helps you understand the right times, places, and situations to introduce signs to your sweetie-peetie. In addition, it helps you determine how many signs to start with; identify when your sweetie-peetie might start signing back; and know why getting family, friends, and caregivers involved is a big bonus.

Recognizing the Right Time to Introduce Signs

Whenever I talk to people about signing with babies, one of the first questions I'm asked is, "When do I start to sign to my baby?" In my mind, I reply, "When do you start to *talk* to your baby?" I only say this in my mind, because if I said it out loud, people would probably get up and leave. But seriously, think about this for a moment: Do you wait until your baby can speak fluently before you speak to him? I hope not. Why would signing with your baby be any different?

Some baby-signing programs do offer concrete suggestions such as, "You should begin to sign with your baby at x months of age," or, "You should begin to sign with baby when baby does x." However, different programs seem to insert different data for the *x*. In my experience that can be confusing for a parent, and I don't care to add to the confusion.

Typically, when other programs offer an age or other indicator to begin signing, they're focusing on a general point at which a baby is developing the necessary cognitive and/or physical skills to sign back. (By the way, as I write these words, I have a baby sleeping down the hall who completely blew all of that general data out of the water when he began signing at 4 months old.) Again I ask, "Do you wait until baby can speak before you speak to baby?" Of course not. Then why should you wait until baby can sign before you sign to baby?

I do feel I should tell you this: The sooner you start teaching baby to sign, the longer you may have to wait for baby to sign back. What I mean is that your baby will not be physically or mentally able to sign for a little while. Again, this is what other programs refer to when they offer specific ages or milestones to look for. These markers are real, even if the experts can't all agree on what they are. At the same time I feel I should tell you this as well: My son Cole, at 18 months, has a sign vocabulary of 102 signs. I know in my heart that that number is as high as it is because he's been surrounded by two parents, two siblings, and a variety of care-givers who have been signing to him since birth.

The better question is not *when,* but *how* to teach baby to sign. I hope you find the answer to the second, much more important question in this book, even if, like most parents, you came looking for the answer to the first. In a nutshell, here's how to teach baby to sign:

✔ Focus on a handful of pertinent signs.

✔ Introduce and reinforce those signs at the right times.

✔ Be consistent.

This book is about discovering how to do those three things — and how to have fun doing them.

Knowing Where to Begin

"So should I start signing every time I say a particular word? Should I only sign at mealtime? Should I make my baby look at me when I sign? Where should I begin?"

All are valid questions, and this section provides the basic answers.

Focus

Many parents in my classes want to begin by signing every word they say to their babies. They find out quickly how many signs they must learn to keep up with their spoken language, and then they become burned out in less than a month because their little darling isn't signing back.

"Why isn't she signing back?" they ask.

"Maybe because you're overwhelming her with too many signs," I say.

Think for a minute about how babies learn to talk. They don't talk in full sentences at first, or even for years. Instead, they start small, with individual words like "da-da" or "ma-ma" or "ba" (which could mean "ball," "bath," or "bird" depending on the context). And that's exactly how you should begin when signing to your baby. Start small.

Pick a handful of signs — say, four or five — to start with. Make sure the signs are of things your baby is interested in and/or that she needs on a daily basis. Watch for items of interest to sign for her. Is her interest in the family dog? The wind? A bus? Books? Take your cue from her. What is part of her daily routine? Milk? Eating? Sleeping? Again, take your cue from her.

Does your family have a dog? A cat? A tank full of fish? Do you ride in the car a lot? Does big sister dance? Big brother play basketball? Daddy play softball? Check out the areas of life that your family is interested and active in, and consider making a handful of those signs your starter repertoire.

If you absolutely have no idea which signs to start with, check out Chapter 4. It covers some handy basic signs, like HELLO, BYE-BYE, MAMA, and DADA.

Look for the right time

The time to introduce the sign for APPLE isn't while your baby is taking a bath. Save APPLE for a mealtime at the kitchen table. But don't follow it with BICYCLE, thinking that, while you've got her attention during mealtime, you might as well introduce what schnookums will see during her afternoon outing at the park. Instead, stick with signs like EAT, MORE, DRINK, FINISHED, and whatever food you're serving (see Chapter 5 for details). Strained CARROTS, anyone?

Likewise, more appropriate signs for bath time are BATH, DUCK (but only if you have a rubber one floating around), WATER, SPLASH, BUBBLES . . . you get the idea. (Chapter 7 provides details on bath-time signs.)

In other words — and this is the all-important take-home point here — remember to sign whatever is appropriate in the situation you're in at that particular moment in time. And just focus on one or two signs. Don't overload.

Consistency counts

Know this tidbit up front: Repetition is important. If you want your little buddy to *get it* — to actually make the connection and understand, for example, that the hand motion you make whenever the family dog walks into the room *means* DOG — you need to sign the word over and over again in context. So if you want to introduce the sign for DOG, then watch for the family pooch to walk into the room, catch your little buddy's attention and say and sign DOG.

And do it with great gusto. If you're excited about signing, then he'll be excited about signing. As you make the sign, say the word loudly or softly or in a silly voice. Whatever it takes to get his attention.

Think about how you try to get your dumpling to smile for a portrait and how crazy the photographer talks in an attempt to get a single smile from your child. You and the photographer talk loudly or softly or in a silly voice, don't you? You use your baby voice. Adults tend to use a different voice, their baby voice, when speaking to infants or toddlers. And kids seem to love it. So while you're signing, apply that same baby voice to get and hold your dumpling's attention.

The sign for DOG, by the way, is in Chapter 9, as are lots of other animal signs. Animals are a gold-mine, high-interest area for kids. Keep that in mind.

Knowing When Baby Might Sign Back

Look for it: The slightest movement of your sweetie's hands can be a sign (pun intended) that she's trying to sign back. Know up front what you're actually looking for, though — you won't see an exact replica of what *your* sign looks like. A sign on her little hands won't look like a sign on your hands. Her tiny size and yet-to-be-developed motor skills will affect her motions.

If you've been signing BALL with your baby, and she moves her hands a bit while looking at a BALL, get excited, praise her, and reinforce the movement by saying, "You signed BALL! Are you ready to play with your BALL?" Be sure to continue signing BALL every time you say it during your praise session. She'll eventually begin to understand that when she moves her hands, it means something.

The younger your baby is when you start signing to her, the longer it will take for her to sign back. Consequently, when you start signing with an older baby, she'll probably respond very quickly.

Making Signing a Family Affair

Signing together as a family is big fun, if I do say so myself. My husband and I have three children. Darby is 4, Aidan Elizabeth is 3, and Cole is 18 months — not necessarily what we planned, but what we joyfully have in our home. And we all participate in signing together.

Recently, for example, while my husband was at a meeting, the girls and I signed through almost an entire meal, with few words spoken. Cole watched and occasionally jumped in with a random sign or a delighted squeal. They've been signing as long as they can remember and have helped teach each other, as well as friends outside the family.

We have video of the girls teaching Cole to sign when he was just weeks old. They're also constantly teaching signs to their baby dolls and stuffed animals. At 18 months, Cole knows 102 signs and 119 spoken words. Keep that nugget in context, though. ***Remember:*** Cole has had four people signing with him since the day he was born. The girls know around 300 signs now and are always asking for more signs.

I believe that signing together forces a family to pay better attention to each other. And, in my humble opinion, it makes you a better parent. If you're constantly watching your child for signs and paying attention to what she's interested in, you learn to read her body signals in addition to her signs. And when you're picking up a particular toy and showing her the sign for it, you're showing her that you're interested in her and that you care about what she's playing with.

Remembering That Caregivers and Friends Are Family, Too

I have a wonderful teenage babysitter named Abby who comes over at least twice a week to help out with the kids (and give mom a break). At one point, Abby showed me a couple of signs and asked if they were correct. I said yep, and she was blown away because my girls, Darby and Aidan Elizabeth, taught those signs to her. Now Abby teaches signs to her friends during lunch.

That's all fine and dandy in itself, but hindsight has shown me this to boot: If you have a babysitter, day-care provider, or friend your sugar pie sees on a regular basis, let him know upfront that you're using sign language with your baby and show him the signs you're working on with your baby. This is especially important if your baby has begun to sign back and will expect any caregiver to know what she's talking and signing about.

Here's a case in point: One time my mom and grandmother were taking care of the girls for a few hours, and I hadn't shown them all the signs the kids might use. Well, at one point Aidan Elizabeth stood outside the pantry and made a sign. My mom and grandma knew she was signing, but they had absolutely no idea *what* she was signing, so they asked Darby to interpret. Because our kitchen's trash can is in the pantry, Darby decided that Aidan Elizabeth was signing DIRTY and that meant trash, so Darby told her DeeDee and Great-Memaw that Aidan Elizabeth had something to throw away. Aidan Elizabeth wasn't even 2 yet, and Darby wasn't yet 3. Later, Darby decided Aidan Elizabeth hadn't been signing for the trash can but *had* been signing COOKIE, and could they both please have one? Smart little cookie, that Darby.

Chapter 3

Warming Up: Signing Boot Camp

* *

In This Chapter

▶ Discovering a few hand shapes commonly used in various signs

▶ Identifying a few rules to get you effectively on your way

* *

*M*any different American Sign Language (ASL) signs share something in common: specific hand shapes. In other words, many signs incorporate the same hand shapes as many other signs. But where you place the common hand shape and what you do with it next is the key to making signs mean different things.

This chapter covers a few of the hand shapes that are commonly used in various different signs. If you get a handle on these hand shapes upfront, you're a bit ahead of the game with various signs. Note, too, that although knowing the ASL alphabet or ASL numbers isn't essential to signing with babies, many ASL hand shapes are based on individual letters or numbers, so I've placed the ASL alphabet in Appendix A and numbers one through ten in Appendix B.

Also important up front is having the right mindset as you prepare to sign with your baby. So, in this chapter, I pass on some of my tips of the trade — some do's and don'ts for you to soak up for success.

Hand Shapes: Not Just for Shadow Puppets Anymore

Remember the days when someone shined a flashlight on the wall in a dark room and you moved your hands to make a duck or a dog or a butterfly in the shadows? The shape you made with your hands was important in creating those shadow puppets. The shape of your hands is also important in creating ASL signs. This section covers a few basic hand shapes that you'll use again and again while creating various signs.

Open-5

The open-5 hand shape is pretty straightforward. Simply hold up your hand, palm away from you, with all five fingers extended and spread apart (see Figure 3-1). As easy as making a quacking duck shadow puppet on the wall, eh?

Figure 3-1: Give me five — an open-5!

Closed-5

The closed-5 hand shape is as simple as the open-5. Just hold up your hand, palm facing away from you, with all five fingers extended and touching each other (see Figure 3-2). Think of the hand shape used for the beauty-queen wave.

Figure 3-2: The closed-5 hand shape. Think "Here she is . . . Miss America!"

Claw-C

I know, *claw* sounds like a bad horror movie. I don't name the hand shapes, okay? I only show them.

To make the claw-C hand shape, follow these directions:

1. **Begin by making the open-5 hand shape (see the directions earlier in this chapter).**

   Note that the open-5 hand shape is also the ASL number five (see Appendix B).

2. **Now slightly bend all five fingers (see Figure 3-3).**

   Looks like a claw, doesn't it? So, yes, it sounds like a bad horror movie, but the name makes sense after all.

Note: Some signers refer to the claw-C hand shape as just a C hand shape. Just one of those tomāto/tomäto things. The sign's the same no matter what you call it.

Figure 3-3: Coming to a theater near you: *Return of the Claw.*

Claw-5

You're probably wondering what happened to claw-2, claw-3, and claw-4. I'll leave that research to you, because they're not pertinent to this book. Regardless, as you may have guessed, this hand shape is similar to the claw-C. ***Note:*** Some ASL signers call this a bent-5. Tomāto/tomäto again . . . it's the same sign either way. Here's how to make the sign:

1. **Begin by making the open-5 hand shape (see the directions earlier in this chapter).**

2. **Without moving your thumb, slightly bend the other four fingers (see Figure 3-4).**

   With the regular ol' claw-C hand shape, you bend your thumb along with your fingers. But with the claw-5 hand shape, your thumb stays extended — not bent.

Figure 3-4: Beware claw-5.

Flat-F

Musically speaking, an F flat is an E. Not so in the world of ASL. In this world, a flat-F is a hand shape, and you make it by following these simple steps:

1. **Begin by making the open-5 hand shape (see the directions earlier in this chapter).**

2. **While holding that position, make an *O* with your index finger and thumb.**

   At this point, you've actually made an ASL letter *F* (see Appendix A).

3. **Extend (straighten) your index finger and thumb only.**

   As you do so, the circle made by these two fingers in the letter *F* is flattened (see Figure 3-5).

Figure 3-5: The flat-F hand shape.

Flat-O

Nope, no musical pun comes to mind for this flat hand shape. So I'll get right to the directions:

1. **Begin by making the closed-5 hand shape (see the directions earlier in this chapter).**

2. **While they're still touching, bend all four fingers and form an *O* with your index finger and thumb.**

   At this point, you've actually made an ASL letter *O* (see Appendix A).

3. **Extend (straighten) all of your fingers and thumb, flattening the circle of your *O* (see Figure 3-6).**

   This hand shape also doubles as a hand puppet with its mouth closed.

Bent-3

We're back to number hand shapes. This one's pretty easy. Here are the directions for the bent-3 hand shape:

1. **Make an ASL three by extending your index finger, middle finger, and thumb (see Appendix B).**

2. **Bend in your two fingers and thumb a bit to make the bent-3 (see Figure 3-7).**

Figure 3-6: The flat-O hand shape.

Figure 3-7: The bent-3 hand shape.

Some Signing Do's and Don'ts

As you prepare to sign with your baby, you need to do more than just figure out how to make and show your baby the signs themselves. You also need to get yourself in the right frame of mind, and the best way to do so is to know and follow some basic rules. Yes, in every arena of life there are rules, things you do and things you don't do. Signing with baby is no exception. In no way does this section encompass *all* the rules for signing with baby, but it does give you a good set to start with.

Do stick with it

Rome wasn't built in a day. Your baby took nine months to get here. Coaching your baby to sign takes time. And keep in mind that each baby develops the ability to sign back at her own individual pace, just as with other aspects of development (like walking, crawling, talking, and such). I can't tell you when your baby will sign back to you. What I can tell you is that the more consistently you sign with her, the more likely you are to get results.

You may get frustrated and begin to wonder if your baby will ever sign back. If you stick with it, the day *will* come. That said, the younger your baby is when you start signing to her, the longer you'll probably have to wait for her first sign back. However, the time you spend signing won't be in vain. She'll understand you before she begins to sign back. And when she does begin to sign back, she'll have a strong foundation already instilled in her. So keep telling yourself, "I'm investing in my baby." And there's no better way to invest.

Do get others involved

Who sees baby on a regular basis? Is it a babysitter, a day-care provider, a grandparent, siblings? Those people need to know which signs you're using with baby and which signs he's signing back. Consistency is vital as you're coaching baby to sign, and if baby's other caregivers are willing to pick up the ball when you aren't around, that's just all the more exposure for baby.

Now many caregivers may choose not to sign with baby due to time constraints or disinterest. Giving them the information is still important, especially when baby begins to sign back. Babies feel frustrated when they're communicating and no one seems to be listening. Recognizing your baby's signs will only make his caregivers' jobs easier. Besides, when they realize that signing works, many caregivers become interested and want to sign with baby as well.

All is not lost if your baby's caregivers ultimately choose not to sign with him. Your influence on him is far greater than anyone else's. If you commit to signing with baby, regardless of what anyone else does or doesn't do, baby will reap the benefits for years to come.

Do look for teachable moments

Teachable moments are those times when baby is most receptive to what you're trying to coach her on. For example, you wouldn't try to coach her on the sign for EAT (see Chapter 5) while baby's in the bathtub. Well, I guess you could be telling her not to EAT the soap, but that's another story. The point is, in order to make the most of the time you invest in coaching baby to sign, be on the lookout for the most opportune settings to do it in.

For example, suppose that you walk into the room to find baby's nose glued to the window. Upon further investigation, you realize she's fascinated by a bird she has discovered on the branch just outside. This is the perfect time to focus on the sign for BIRD (see Chapter 9). "Do you see that BIRD? Isn't that a pretty BIRD? What does the BIRD say? Chirp, chirp, chirp!"

 So be on the lookout. When baby is interested in an object, that's the best time to show her the sign for it. If you don't happen to know the sign for that particular object, use the sign WHAT, found in Chapter 1.

Do continue signing after baby speaks

One of my greatest frustrations comes when parents stop signing with their baby simply because baby has started to speak. I'm also saddened when parents comment, "That's so cool. I wish I had signed with my kids. Now it's too late." These parents usually have kids who are around age 2. Usually my response is, "You still have time. Want to come to one of my classes?"

The benefits of coaching your child to sign don't disappear simply because he can suddenly express himself with words. True, signing bridges a communication gap with your baby while he's too young to speak and helps you understand what he's thinking and feeling. But your quest to know what's going on in his mind doesn't stop the minute he begins to speak, and many times children can find a way to express themselves through signs in ways they can't through words.

Do have fun

If you're not having fun, chances are your baby isn't having fun either. Signing with baby is about communicating with her, show-ing her that you care about her thoughts and needs, and reducing the stress and frustration that baby's inability to communicate can lead to. These are all *good* things, and you ought to enjoy the process.

Ever heard the saying "If it's not fun, it's not worth doing"? That's truly the case for signing with your baby. If you're not enjoying it, here's what to do: Take a step back, take a deep breath, and reread this chapter's list of do's and don'ts to make sure you're following them, especially the next one, "Don't overwhelm baby." Nine times out of ten, if you're frustrated trying to coach baby to sign and seeing no results, the reason is because your baby is overwhelmed by too many signs.

Don't overwhelm baby

This is probably the most common mistake I've seen parents make when they're coaching their baby to sign. They find a book like this one, get to know all the signs as fast as they can, and try to use them with baby all at once. Baby can't get to know these signs as quickly as you can, and if you give your baby more than he can handle, he'll likely tune out.

So how much is too much? A good guideline, at least as you're getting started, is to focus on five or six signs. Be choosey when you pick these signs. They should be things that are a big part of baby's life, including things that baby really needs, like MILK (see Chapter 5), as well as things that baby really loves, like his favorite BALL (see Chapter 10).

When baby begins to sign one of these five or six initial signs, you can add a new one. So, theoretically, at any given time you should only be working with the signs baby already knows and can sign, plus five or six that you're trying to coach him on.

By the way, this approach also means you don't have to feel overwhelmed. You really don't have to get proficient with every sign in ASL or even every sign in this book right away. You just have to keep pace with baby. Trust me, you can do it.

Don't expect perfection

You don't expect perfection from baby when it comes to oral communication, right? In other words, you don't sit around expecting her to say "mommy" or "daddy" with perfect diction the first time she speaks. In fact, the first time one of her gurgles even comes close to sounding like "ma-ma" or "da-da" you're jumping for joy, pulling out the memory book, and calling all the grandparents.

So have the same realistic expectations with baby and signing. The first time your baby signs MILK (see Chapter 5), she probably won't get it just right. In fact, it may be quite a while before she does. That's okay. The goal when signing with baby is communication. If you know what baby is trying to sign, if you understand the need or desire she's trying to express, then you've achieved this goal.

Keep in mind that it's not so important to correct baby when her signs are not just so, but it *is* important to continue modeling proper sign technique. Consider this example from oral communication: Baby may call water "wa-wa," but you know she means water. You let her know you understand her, but you continue to say "water," and eventually she says "water" too. Do the same thing with signing: When you realize that your baby is trying to communicate a sign back to you (and believe me, you'll know), don't get caught up in whether or not she does it just right. Applaud baby's attempts. Encourage her by letting her know that you understand her. Don't worry about correcting her. But continue to model the sign properly. The rest will take care of itself.

Don't be surprised when baby takes off

Coaching baby to sign takes time. It may seem like it's taking forever for him to sign back for the first time. It may feel that way again before the next sign comes. But take heart; it won't always be this way.

I have a cousin who diligently worked with his baby to walk. He and his wife held her hands and guided her, encouraging her to take a few steps back and forth between them — you know the routine. Then one day, when my cousin picked up his little one from day care, her caregivers reported, "She's been walking all day." She hasn't crawled since.

The same thing will happen when you work with your baby to sign. The first few signs will come at a snail's pace. Then one day he'll suddenly begin signing back every sign you've been trying to coach him on. For a little while, you'll even have to work hard to figure out new signs fast enough to show him. Then the pace will slow down. Then it'll take off again. Coaching baby to sign will be filled with stops and starts, slow periods and fast ones. Just remember, if you want him to take off, if you want to make it to one of those fast-paced stages (and you do want to make it there), you have to remain diligent during the slow times.

Don't listen to the skeptics

Life is full of skeptics — the glass-is-half-empty crowd. As you begin to sign with your baby, the skeptics will come out of the woodwork. They may be your in-laws or even your own parents. They may be your best friends or complete strangers. The skeptic may even be your spouse. All those skeptics will roll their eyes. They'll say you're crazy. They'll warn you that your baby will never learn to speak.

The skeptics will be wrong. Let them roll their eyes. It's not crazy to want to communicate with your baby as soon as possible. It's not crazy to want to reduce the stress in your baby's life. And know that not only will your baby learn to speak, but he'll also probably be a step ahead of his non-signing peers (see Chapter 1).

You're a hero. You're doing the right thing for your baby. Don't let anyone tell you otherwise.

Part II
Ready, Set, Sign!

The 5th Wave   By Rich Tennant

"You've either lost the lid to the blender, or you're introducing mealtime signs to the baby."

In this part . . .

You've made the decision to sign with your baby, so you've assumed the ready, set position. Thing is, you're stuck at the starting line because you have no idea *what* to sign, let alone where to do it and how to make the signs themselves.

Well, fret not. Part II offers you some great starting places. Here, you find some basic signs, signs for mealtime, safety signs, and signs for bed and bath. These signs pertain to the daily necessities of baby's life. Because of the nearly constant day-to-day repetition of the activities related to these signs, one of them may very well become the first one that your baby signs back.

As an added bonus, all the signs in this part directly help you communicate with baby about his care and well-being. And don't even worry about how to make these signs. Every sign presented in this book comes with detailed, illustrated, step-by-step instructions. You'll be signing right away — and baby will be signing along before you know it!

Chapter 4

Signing 101: Some Basic Signs

*I*n our busy lives, coming and going are continuous actions for all of us, including babies and toddlers. Most little ones are constantly telling one caregiver good-bye and another hello as their parents rush off to work or the gym or wherever. But no matter where junior is at the moment, he usually has the same people and everyday things on his mind. Those people are his family, and those everyday things are getting his diaper changed, getting used to going to the potty, and getting his cup filled.

In this chapter, I cover some signs you and your little one can use as you drop him off, pick him up, and meet folks out in the world. I also cover some signs that communicate who's who in the family and what's what in the business of diapers, potties, and cups. In other words, I explain a few basic signs that any caregiver can use with your baby throughout the day, night, or weekend (oh, to be so lucky).

Meeting and Greeting: You Say Good-Bye, and I Say Hello . . .

Babies and toddlers are constantly attempting to connect with others around them, whether it's mom, a friend, or a stranger in the grocery store. You can use the signs in this section to help junior, you, and whoever else know what he's really saying. After all, a parent does need to monitor these things.

Hello

Well, you get lucky on the sign for HELLO. Much of American Sign Language (ASL) is made up of natural gestures we already know and love. HELLO is a great example of natural-gesture-turned-ASL.

Be sure to introduce the sign HELLO in a natural context and setting, like when you're at the grocery store and your munchkin notices a smiley lady in the cereal aisle. Catch your munchkin's eye and say, "See the nice lady? Let's say HELLO," and then make the sign like this:

1. **Make an ASL *B* by holding your four fingers straight up and laying your thumb across your palm.**

   You can find the ASL alphabet in Appendix A.

2. **While still holding your fingers in the *B* shape, place your index finger at your temple.**

3. **Move your hand out as if you're a soldier saluting someone (see Figure 4-1).**

See? Signing isn't as difficult as you thought.

Figure 4-1: HELLO, friend.

Always reinforce a sign by repeating yourself as often as possible after first introducing it. In the case of HELLO, for example, after first introducing the sign, wait a minute and then do it again. If you're in the grocery store and you just said HELLO to a nice lady in the cereal aisle, move on to the next aisle, catch your child's eye a second time, say "Let's say HELLO again!" and make the sign very excitedly to the next smiley person you see.

Bye-bye

Is there anything cuter than a baby waving bye-bye? Not much. And as luck would have it, the sign for BYE-BYE is the same natural gesture we all know and love. So whether you and your baby are saying good-bye to Dad, the babysitter, or the smiley lady in the cereal aisle, mention to munchkin what's going on — "BYE-BYE, nice lady in the cereal aisle!" — while simultaneously making the following sign:

1. **Place your hand parallel to your body, fingertips pointing up.**

2. **As a whole, move your fingers down and up (see Figure 4-2).**

Figure 4-2: Buh-bye.

That's it. You've just signed BYE-BYE. You already knew some ASL — you just didn't know you knew it!

I love you

Seeing your baby sign I LOVE YOU is heart melting. I should know: The "I love you, Mommy" sidebar in this chapter is about my own son signing I LOVE YOU.

This sign is a combination of the ASL letters *I*, *L*, and *Y*. (To find more on the ASL alphabet, turn to Appendix A.)

Say and sign I LOVE YOU with your baby — aw shucks, with *every-one* in your family — as often as possible. Here are the magic steps to melting hearts:

1. **Put your little finger up, with the rest of your fingers in a fist.**
2. **Put your index finger up, too.**
3. **While your little finger and index fingers are still up, move your thumb out (see Figure 4-3).**

   Been to a heavy-metal concert lately? Probably not, being that baby now has a monopoly over your nights and week-ends and, well, your social life in general. But I digress. If you've *ever* been to a heavy-metal concert, yep, this is the exact same sign rock stars use during their power ballads to profess their love to their fans.

Figure 4-3: Awww, I LOVE YOU, too.

I love you, Mommy

When my son Cole was 10 months old, I was putting him down for a nap one day. As I was laying him down, I said and signed, "I LOVE YOU, Cole." To my utmost sur-prise, he shook his little hand back and forth in an attempt of I LOVE YOU and then signed MOMMY. Needless to say, I had tears in my eyes as I tiptoed out of his room. No doubt he'll be a heartbreaker someday (grin and sigh).

Thank you

All parents want their kids to be polite, and the sooner you begin teaching yours to say THANK YOU, the better. Being too young to talk is no excuse for bad manners, which is why the sign THANK YOU comes in handy.

Say that little dumpling has let you know one way or another that she'd like her teddy bear. You plop down on your knees beside her bed, lift the quilt that's dragging the floor, and find the bear alongside yesterday's bunched-up socks. As you hand the bear to her, be sure to ask her to say THANK YOU for your efforts and show her how with this sign:

1. **Place the tips of your fingers on your chin.**

2. **In one gesture, move your hand down with your fingertips pointing away from your chin (see Figure 4-4).**

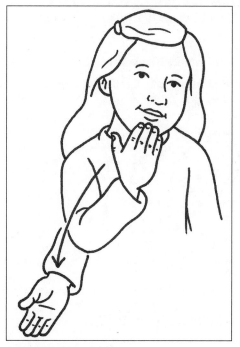

Figure 4-4: THANK YOU!

Who Are You Again?

Parents are always anxious for their children to say their first word. But one of parenting's many ironies is that in a few years, those same parents are always longing, instead, for their children to *puh-leez* be quiet. But that's off the point du jour.

The point is that two of the first words children usually speak are *mama* and *dada*. So why not give them a head start by using the signs for those words? In this section, I show you how to make those signs, as well as the signs for a few other special people in your child's life.

Mama

Seeing their babies sign MAMA for the very first time makes grown women grin and sends a shot of love right through their hearts. You moms out there will definitely want to experience this feeling, so frequently introduce yourself to your baby while simultaneously making this sign:

1. **Spread your fingers like you've just counted to five.**

2. **While still holding your five fingers up, place your thumb on your chin (see Figure 4-5).**

Figure 4-5: Hi there, MAMA!

Note that the MAMA sign works for Mama, Mommy, Mom, Mother, or whatever term you use for the maternal unit of the family.

Dada

Although seeing your child sign MAMA for the first time is heart-warming, seeing your child sign DADA can actually draw tears. Trust me. I've seen it with my own eyes. You dads out there will definitely want some of this for yourself, so frequently introduce yourself to your baby while simultaneously making this sign:

1. **Spread your fingers like you've just counted to five.**

2. **While still holding your five fingers up, place your thumb on your forehead (see Figure 4-6).**

Figure 4-6: DADA!

Note that the DADA sign works for Dada, Daddy, Dad, Father, or whatever term you use for the paternal unit of the family.

Baby

One of the neat things about using sign language is that, after your child learns the sign for a word, she can sometimes use it in a totally different context. Take BABY, for example. When your baby gets a handle on signing BABY to refer to herself, she can also use the sign to let you know that she sees someone else's baby at, say, the day-care center or even that she wants her baby doll. Same word, same sign, different uses.

So whenever the situation applies, say and sign BABY to let your sweetie know that she can use the sign in many scenarios. Here's how to sign the word:

1. **Cradle your arms at waist level.**

2. **Rock them back and forth (see Figure 4-7).**

Figure 4-7: Who's your BABY?

Grandma

Whether you call her Grandma, Granny, Memaw, DeeDee, or Nana, she's probably an important part of your child's life. That's as good a reason as any to include the sign for her in your child's repertoire. The term you use is totally up to you, but always follow it with this sign:

1. **Make the sign for MAMA (see the "Mama" section).**

2. **Move your hand out and down, stopping for a short time at 90 degrees and 180 degrees (see Figure 4-8).**

Figure 4-8: Please, GRANDMA?

Now go call your mother or mother-in-law and tell her you're teaching your baby to sign GRANDMA. You'll be a big hit, and the entire family will be focused on your signing baby at the next family gathering.

Grandpa

As if GRANDPA needed another thing to be proud of, watching his grandkid use the sign for GRANDPA is totally endearing. Here's how to make this sign, which applies no matter whether you call him Grandpa, Gramps, Papaw, Pappy, or even Pampu:

1. **Make the sign for DADA (see the "Dada" section).**

2. **Move your hand out and down, stopping for a short time at 90 degrees and 180 degrees (see Figure 4-9).**

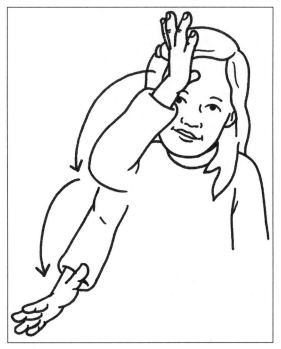

Figure 4-9: Signing for GRAMPS.

A Few Everyday Needs

I hear ya: Signs for family members are cute and everything, but what about signs to help make your life easier (like reduce screaming fits, for example)? Yep, those kinds of signs do exist, and I'm here to please.

Your baby or toddler probably has a few things on his mind regularly, like what's in his diaper, or whether the feeling he's experiencing means he needs to go visit the potty, or where his cup is at the moment (and whether he can get it filled). The three simple signs in this section relate to those things and will get you and your baby on the right track with two-way communication beyond "waaaaaah!" Good luck.

Diaper

One of the things babies often fuss about is the condition of their diapers. How fantastic would it be to have your baby sign DIAPER *before* she starts screaming? It is possible, my friend, so regularly talk with your child about the condition of her diaper while simultaneously signing the magic word like this:

1. **Make an *L* with both hands by pointing your index fingers up and holding your thumbs out to the side.**

   To see the entire ASL alphabet, turn to Appendix A.

2. **On both hands, close your index finger and thumb together.**

3. **Place your hands near the top of where a diaper would be, around the waist area.**

4. **Open and close your fingers and thumbs two or three times (see Figure 4-10).**

Figure 4-10: Change my DIAPER, please.

Potty

Signing for a DIAPER change is a wonderful thing, but signing for the POTTY is even better. Just think, no more diapers to clean up. . . . Pardon me, I lost myself for a second, dreaming of that glorious day.

Note that if your baby is too young to use the potty yet, you can always introduce the sign anyway, just so baby can hear the word and see the sign regularly. And if baby has a big brother, regularly say and sign POTTY with big brother while in the baby's presence to keep driving home the point of the potty. In other words, in this particular case it's okay to have a potty mouth. Say and sign POTTY all the time. The payoff down the road is huge.

Here's how to walk the walk and sign the sign:

1. **Make a fist.**

2. **While your hand is still in a fist, make an ASL letter *T* by placing your thumb between your index and middle fingers.**

   You can check out the entire ASL alphabet in Appendix A.

3. **Shake your hand back and forth a few times (see Figure 4-11).**

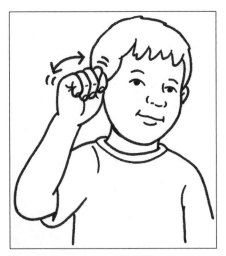

Figure 4-11: Time to go POTTY.

Cup

CUP is one of those handy multipurpose signs — useful for all types of cup situations. The CUP sign will come in handy during your little one's transition from baby bottle to big-boy cup. And the same CUP sign can be used for communication when your little one is trying to get into Mommy or Daddy's cup. Additionally, your baby can use the CUP sign to actually tell you when he's thirsty and wants his cup. (You can find signs for things to go in cups in Chapter 5.)

1. **Form the ASL letter *C* by rounding your fingers and thumb.**

   In other words, make an *O* with your fingers and thumb and then open up a little space between them. (See Appendix A for the whole ASL alphabet.)

2. **Place your *C* hand on your opposite hand's open palm (see Figure 4-12).**

Figure 4-12: May I have my CUP?

Chapter 5

Eat, Baby, Eat!
Mealtime Signs

*I*deally, having the entire family sit down together for dinner can be a delightful end to a busy day. But in reality, it can be more a source of major frustration than relaxation. Mealtime can become crazy-baby time, with food flying, cups spilling, and mouths intensely screaming — on both your and little darling's part. And then there's the mess to deal with afterwards.

This chapter provides the info you need to show that sweet baby how to sign what she wants or needs instead of covering your face with mushed carrots. I mean, granted, it's great that she has a strong opinion, but why not let her express it in the toy room instead of the highchair? At the very least, the outcome will be easier to clean up.

Magic Signs for Mealtime

The best time to introduce signs related to mealtime is while you're sitting at the table during a regular, routine meal. Don't set up a formal lesson or formal setting for the occasion. Just be casual and introduce the signs naturally in the course of your standard conversation with baby.

In this section, I cover four signs for communicating words that are common during mealtime.

Eat

So you're sitting on your last nerve in the playroom while Mighty Lungs is screaming at the top of his lungs beside you. You simply can't figure out what he wants. He swats away his teddy bear and favorite toys when you offer them up. He's not sitting in a poopy diaper. He's not cold and doesn't have a boo-boo. What? *What?*

You notice that he stops his waaaahs as he spots a Cheerio on the floor. Before you can intervene, he picks it up and pops it in his mouth. Momentary bliss and enchantment ensue as he looks around for more yummy floor nuggets, but upon finding none, he starts screaming again. Duh. You realize that he's probably hungry, so you scoop him up and head straight to the kitchen for a snack.

There's an easier way — trust me. The sign for EAT will help your baby tell you when he wants to eat so that you won't have to decipher screaming. The sign is simple to make, like this:

1. **Make a flat-O hand shape by first forming an *O* with your fingers and thumb and then flattening them out so that they look like a deflated balloon.**

   You can find the ASL alphabet in Appendix A.

2. **Touch your fingertips to your mouth repeatedly (see Figure 5-1).**

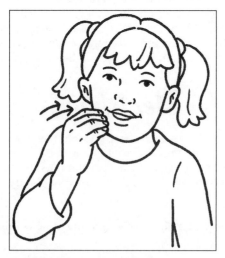

Figure 5-1: I'm ready to EAT, mama dear.

As you're first introducing a new sign to your baby, repeat it often. For example, use the sign for EAT any time you're talking to your baby about food, and specifically sign EAT every time you say the word: "Are you hungry? Do you want to EAT?", "Would you like to EAT some bananas?", or "Mommy is EATing, do you want to EAT, too?"

Drink

No matter what her preference — milk, juice, or water — when she wants her DRINK, she wants it *now*. (Ask me how I know this.) Show her how to sign DRINK to get what she wants more quickly and with a lot less frustration:

1. **Form an ASL *C* with one hand as if you're holding a drink.**

   See Appendix A for the ASL alphabet.

2. **Mimic drinking by bringing your hand to your mouth and tilting it several times (see Figure 5-2).**

Figure 5-2: A DRINK sure would be nice right about now.

By the way, I cover the sign for MILK later in this chapter. The sign for WATER is covered in Chapter 7's discussion on scrubbing in the tub. (If you're interested in finding the sign for JUICE, check out Chapter 17 to find a list of other signing resources.)

More

Many of your darlin's frustrations stem from wanting MORE of something. And I'm not just talking about your spouse wanting more. Your *other* darlin' wants MORE, too — MORE to eat, MORE to drink, MORE swinging time, MORE bubbles — and he gets frustrated when you can't make the connection. The sign for MORE can come in handy several times a day, in countless scenarios. Here's how to make the sign:

1. **Using both hands, make two flat-O hand shapes (see Chapter 3).**

2. **Repeatedly touch the fingertips of both hands (see Figure 5-3).**

Figure 5-3: MORE, please.

Finished

When your baby's done eating, do you usually have a tyrant on your hands, kicking and screaming while trying to get out of her high chair? Such a joy.

Granted, she's too young to be able to say, "May I please be excused?" But even though the words aren't there yet, she can certainly let you know she's FINISHED by using the sign. During every meal, be sure to ask your baby, "Are you FINISHED?" and simultaneously show her how to make the sign, like this:

1. **Place both hands in the air, near your shoulders, fingertips pointing up, palms facing away from your body.**

2. **Rotate your hands at the wrist so that your palms face your body.**

3. **Repeat the rotation several times (see Figure 5-4).**

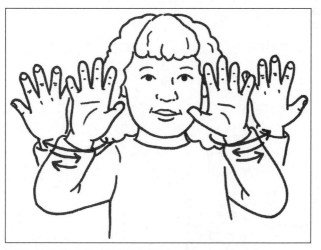

Figure 5-4: I'm full and FINISHED, thank you very much.

Growing Food, Part 1: Fruits

A tasty alternative to sugary snacks, fruit is a fantastic way to bring growing food into your baby's world without her realizing it's good for her. If you're introducing fruits to your baby, why not sign the words while saying them? In time, your little one will be able to let you know which fruit she wants as a snack or with her meal. In this section, I cover a few favorite fruit signs. Say and sign them whenever the opportunity presents itself. Then rinse and repeat.

Apple

She's probably a bit too young to take an APPLE to her teacher, but she probably loves seeing that bright, shiny, round, red thing you munch on regularly. Be ready to define her curiosity with the sign for APPLE:

1. **Form an ASL letter *A* with one hand by making a fist and placing your thumb against your index finger.**

   You can find the ASL alphabet in Appendix A.

2. **While your hand is still in that position, place your thumb on your cheek and twist your hand forward (see Figure 5-5).**

Figure 5-5: An APPLE a day. . . .

Banana

Bananas are a great finger food for junior, and the sign also works great when you're visiting the monkeys at the zoo. (Check out Chapter 9 for animal signs.) The bonus is that the sign for BANANA is fun to make. Check it out:

1. **Raise one index finger, with the tip pointing to the sky.**

   Pretend this finger is a banana.

2. **With your opposite hand, make the movements of peeling a banana, starting at your fingertip and moving down and out (see Figure 5-6).**

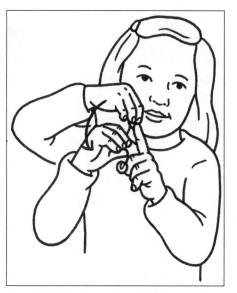

Figure 5-6: Monkey see, monkey do; may I have a BANANA, too?

Grapes

Yum! Grapes are a delicious addition to any healthy diet. And kids love them. Of course, when you give grapes to your little sweetheart, don't forget to cut them into small pieces to avoid the choking-hazard thing.

Whenever you're cutting up grapes for a salad, snack, or meal, or you're popping them into your own mouth, talk about them to your baby and make the sign for GRAPES like this:

1. **Raise one elbow to shoulder height, and allow the rest of your arm to dangle rag-doll style.**

   Your dangling arm represents the vine that grapes grow on.

2. **Place the fingertips of your opposite hand facedown in the area below the wrist of your dangling arm.**

3. **Bounce the fingers down to your dangling hand (see Figure 5-7).**

Figure 5-7: Bear the GRAPES or bear my wrath.

Peach

Even if you aren't from the Peach State, Georgia, peaches are delicious and perfect to give both yourself and your baby. Whenever you're dishing them out, talk the talk and walk the walk. In other words, say and sign the word PEACH:

1. **Make a relaxed-5 hand shape by first forming an open-5 shape (see Chapter 3) and then loosely bending your fingers over.**

2. **While your hand is still in that position, lightly brush your fingertips to your cheek several times (see Figure 5-8).**

Berry

Blueberries, strawberries, raspberries, blackberries. . . . Many kids love them, and the sign for BERRY can be used for all of them. Isn't ASL great? You make the sign like so:

1. **Make a flat-O hand shape (see Chapter 3) with one hand and extend the index finger of the other hand.**

2. **Now gently twist your flat-O hand on the tip of the opposite index finger as if you were twisting the stem off the cherry (see Figure 5-9).**

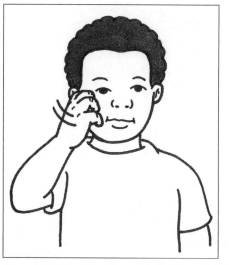

Figure 5-8: If Brad's a Pitt, can he still be a PEACH?

Figure 5-9: BERRY good!

Growing Food, Part II: Veggies

Everyone loves fruit — so much so, in fact, that veggies get a bad rap in comparison. But vegetables are also an essential part of a good diet. Introducing them to your baby is a good thing, and so is leading by example (meaning eat *your* veggies, too, and for goodness' sake don't grimace while doing it). Say and sign various veggies whenever the opportunity presents itself. This section provides a few signs to help you get started.

Carrots

Carrots are full of fantastic fuel for your growing baby. Careful, though, too many and your baby gets an orange tint to her skin, making her look like the offspring of an Oompa Loompa. But that's off the point, which is to sign CARROT whenever you offer one to your baby:

1. **Make an ASL letter *S* (see Appendix A) by forming a fist with your thumb wrapped around the outside of your fingers.**

   Pretend you're holding a carrot in your fist. There you go. That's the position you need to hold.

2. **Move your fist all the way to your mouth as if you're eating up a carrot (see Figure 5-10).**

Figure 5-10: Care for a CARROT?

Peas

Peas are a staple at many meals. They're easy to prepare, fairly inexpensive, and an excellent growing food. Likewise, the sign for PEAS is easy to make, totally free, and an excellent communication tool:

1. **Extend both index fingers.**

2. **Use the tip of one index finger to touch the side of the other index finger several times, moving from knuckle to fingertip. (see Figure 5-11).**

   This motion indicates peas in a pod.

Figure 5-11: Mmm, PEAS.

Corn

Golden corn. Baby corn. Sweet corn. Corn on the cob. However you dish it up, let your little nibblet know what he's getting ready to savor. Catch his eye, say, "Look at this yummy CORN. We're going to EAT some CORN," and sign the pertinent words. Here's how to sign the word du jour:

1. **Pretend you're holding a cob of corn in your hands.**

   In other words, hold your hands out, palms facing each other, with your fingers bent as if grasping the ends of the cob.

2. **While keeping that position, move your hands to your mouth.**

3. **Now turn your hands like you're turning a corn cob as you eat it (see Figure 5-12).**

Figure 5-12: CORN is a fun sign to make.

Lettuce

Lots of people have salads with their meals — both at home and at restaurants. Next time you're enjoying one, take the opportunity to let baby know what salad is primarily made up of — LETTUCE. Point out all that green stuff, say, "Look at all this LETTUCE! Do you want to try some LETTUCE?", and make the sign like this:

1. **Imagine your head is a head of lettuce.**

   Okay, granted, you don't actually have to *do* anything for the first step except get yourself in a vegetable state of mind.

2. **Touch the heel of your palm to your head a couple of times (see Figure 5-13).**

   With this motion, your hand is representing leaves of lettuce.

Figure 5-13: That salad sure is full of LETTUCE!

Got Dairy?

Dairy products provide much-needed calcium and nutrients for your rapidly growing baby, and, fortunately, many ways are available for your sweetie to get her daily quota. In this section, I provide the signs for two simple options — good ol' milk and cheese — because these two items probably have a permanent home in your fridge and are a daily part of your baby's life.

Milk

Whether it's mommy's milk or formula, MILK is the first drink for babies. After babies are weaned from their bottle or their mother's breast, regular cow's MILK is the next thing most babies drink. So MILK is also a common introductory sign. And, lucky you, the sign for breast, formula, or cow's MILK is the same. Use it every time your baby takes a bottle or has a drink of MILK:

1. **Imagine that a cow is standing right beside you.**

   Okay, you don't actually have to *do* anything for the first step except get yourself in a Farmer Brown state of mind. Think overalls, plaid shirt, and mud boots. And go ahead, visualize a toothpick between your teeth.

2. **Open and close the fist of one hand several times, little finger closest to the floor (see Figure 5-14).**

   Yes, you're pretending that you're milking a cow. Moooo. (And if you're now totally in a farming frame of mind, pour that child some milk, find a storybook on farm animals, and read it together while baby enjoys her dairy. You can find the sign for COW and other farm animals in Chapter 9.)

Figure 5-14: Moo! MILK comes from cows.

Cheese

Most kids love CHEESE on *anything*. Help your baby ask for CHEESE when he wants it by showing him the sign while talking it up: "I love CHEESE! I'm putting CHEESE on my sandwich. Do you want a slice of CHEESE, too?" Making the sign is easy:

1. **Place your palms together, fingers touching opposite wrists.**

2. **Rub the heels of your palms together (see Figure 5-15).**

   To visualize this sign, think of squishing cheese in your hands. Sounds like a fun thing to do, right? My kids sure think so.

Grains = Vroom + Vroom

Children need grains to grow and to boost their energy levels. I know, I hear ya: "But keeping up with them is tough enough *without* boosting their energy levels!" Okay, on second thought, maybe children *don't* need grains in their diets.

Figure 5-15: CHEESE, please!

You know I'm kidding. Grains are a staple, so showing your munchkin how to sign common grain foods is smart and practical. In this section, I give you three starter signs that you and your baby can get a lot of mileage out of: CEREAL, CRACKER, and SPAGHETTI.

Cereal

Infant rice and infant oatmeal cereal quickly progress to little round circles of cereal, but the sign stays the same. Take the opportunity to say and sign CEREAL whenever your little one is slurping (and eventually crunching on) this common breakfast food. Three steps and you're there:

1. **Cup one hand as though it's a bowl.**

2. **Make an ASL C with the opposite hand (see Appendix A).**

3. **Extend the index and middle fingers of your opposite hand to act as a spoon.**

4. **Bring your fingertips from the cupped hand to your mouth as if you're eating cereal (see Figure 5-16).**

Figure 5-16: CEREAL — quite possibly the world's perfect breakfast.

Cracker

Kids can drive you CRACKERS, but they also like to eat CRACKERS. Sometimes they do both at the same time. Hopefully, you have more times of the latter than the former with your little bundle of joy.

Crackers are a great and portable snack, so show your baby how to sign for them. Think of it: No matter where you are — at home, a friend's house, the park, church, the mall — your baby will be able to efficiently communicate her snacking desire, and you won't have to work through a frustrating set of 20 questions to figure out why the crying fit. Here's the sign for CRACKER:

1. **Cross one arm over your chest.**

2. **Make a fist with your opposite hand.**

3. **Use the fist to tap the elbow of the crossed arm (see Figure 5-17).**

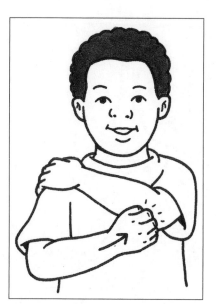

Figure 5-17: Baby want a CRACKER?

Spaghetti

A small child eating spaghetti or other pastas is a joy to watch (well, as long as the spaghetti isn't attached to a sauce that stains). And kids get as much joy doing the eating as the parents do the watching. In other words, spaghetti is fun food, which makes it common food in households with youngsters. If it's on the weekly menu at your house, sign SPAGHETTI while you're all yucking it up at the dinner table:

1. **Extend the little fingers on both hands.**

2. **Move the fingers in circles in opposite directions (see Figure 5-18).**

   The little fingers represent the thin consistency of spaghetti.

Figure 5-18: SPAGHETTI is fun to eat *and* sign.

Fun Food! Desserts

As much as parents want their children to have healthy eating habits, a little bit of dessert thrown in doesn't hurt anything. Because cake and cookies are common desserts for babies and toddlers, both at home and at parties, this section covers those signs.

Cake

It's Timmy's first birthday. Grandma and Grandpa are on hand to help celebrate. They've worn him out playing games and reading interactive books. He's worn himself out tearing open his gifts and showing off his new skill — walking. But he can't plop down for a nap yet because Mom just lit the candle on his birthday cake. Big occasion. Important dessert. Sign away:

1. **Make an ASL letter *C* with one hand (see Appendix A).**

2. **Rest the pinkie of your *C* hand on your opposite hand, which is flat out and palm up.**

3. **Move your *C* hand across the flat hand in the shape of an *X* as if cutting a slice of cake (see Figure 5-19).**

Figure 5-19: Nothin' says "special occasion" like a piece of CAKE.

Cookie

As much as little sweetheart likes cake, cookies can be much less mess for you to clean up. They're quick, easy, portable desserts that come in lots of varieties, so they're commonly found in the homes of families. That makes them a prime candidate for signing with baby. Here's how to sign COOKIE:

1. **Hold out one hand, palm open and facing up.**

   This hand is mimicking rolled-out cookie dough.

2. **Form a *C* hand shape with your other hand (see Appendix A).**

   This hand is mimicking a cookie cutter.

3. **Lower your *C* hand, fingers and thumb pointing down, onto the palm of your opposite hand and then twist, raise, and lower your *C* hand again (see Figure 5-20).**

   Think in terms of using a cookie cutter to cut out cookie shapes.

Figure 5-20: May I have a COOKIE?

If you've just read this chapter all the way through, I'm sure you're hungry. I know I am. So, go and fix yourself — and your baby — a little snack.

Chapter 6

Signs to Help Keep Baby Safe and Sound

In This Chapter

▶ Keeping baby safe with signs

▶ Helping baby express his feelings and emotions

As a parent, I've never been naïve enough to think I wouldn't have to make a rush trip to the emergency room or doctor's office. However, I didn't realize just how *often* I'd need to make such a trip. Here's a quickie sampling: a rock in the nose (3-year-old), a broken nose (15-month-old), a gash in the forehead (2-year-old), as well as various nasty ear infections and bouts of continual vomiting and sky-high fevers. And I've only been a parent for four years.

You may be laughing, or horrified — but no matter how safe you try to keep your kids, you may be right where I am soon enough. Up front and beforehand, be aware of the amount of stress that emergency trips create within the family system. I've found that on several occasions, signing helped out tremendously.

But emergencies aside, the signs covered in this chapter can help you and your baby communicate effectively during various trials and tribulations of everyday life. You can use these signs for an ounce of prevention as well as to help your baby understand what she's feeling in various situations.

Ounce-of-Prevention Signs

Every day is a trial when you have a baby in the house. As a parent, you have to stay on guard constantly to ensure that little sweetums doesn't hurt himself. Regularly communicating safety words is good preventive maintenance. Whenever you do so, I recommend that you also *sign* the safety words. In time, maybe your little one will start signing the words, too — which will benefit you in all kinds of trying situations. This section covers some handy safety signs to keep in your back pocket for use at a moment's notice.

Hot

So your baby is fascinated by the fire in the fireplace. Aren't we all? But how do you explain to baby not to touch a fire? After all, the fire is very pretty and he likes to touch pretty things.

The best way I've found to combat that potentially dangerous curiosity is to proactively teach the appropriate sign, which will help later, just as he's reaching for the fireplace. The appropriate sign is HOT, and here's how to make it:

1. **Make an ASL letter *C* with either hand (see Appendix A).**

2. **While holding the *C* position, place your fingertips just under your nose, and your thumb tip just under your bottom lip.**

3. **Quickly move your hand away from your mouth and twist your wrist so that your fingertips are facing away from your body (see Figure 6-1).**

   Think in terms of quickly turning away something that's hot.

Figure 6-1: That's HOT.

Cold

Your little neck of the woods just had its first big snowfall of the season. Woo-hoo! So you take baby over to the window and show her the pretty, white stuff in the backyard. You then tell her that she gets to go outside to play in the snow. She gets *really* psyched and immediately makes a beeline for the back door.

Not so fast, kiddo. You scramble to catch her and explain, "It's COLD out there! We'll get very COLD if we go outside without our coats! Let's get ready to go outside in the COLD!" Sign the word COLD each time you say it:

1. **Make fists with both hands and hold them at shoulder level.**

2. **Shake your fists and arms as if you're shivering in the cold (see Figure 6-2).**

Figure 6-2: Talk about COLD!

 A great way to teach your baby the difference between HOT and COLD is to use a cold pack and a heating pad (set on low) or a warm pack. Hold the cold pack in baby's hand and sign and say "COLD!" Do the same thing with the sign for HOT. Any time you're around HOT and/or COLD things, use the opportunity to show the sign. Teachable moments may be during extreme HOT or COLD weather or if the bath water is one extreme or the other. Just make sure that what you're having your baby touch isn't *so* extreme that it'll hurt her.

Stop

STOP is a fabulous sign to have in your back pocket, because you can use it for many situations. I recently used STOP when my 15-month-old son headed for the street during a play date. I yelled "STOP!" and when he turned to see why Mommy was yelling, I signed STOP as I ran to scoop him up. Here's how to make the sign:

1. **Hold out one hand as if preparing to shake hands with someone.**

2. **Hold out your opposite hand so that the palm is facing up.**

3. **Use the edge of Step 1's hand to come down sharply on your opposite hand's palm (see Figure 6-3).**

Figure 6-3: STOP!

Wait

Waiting is hard for little people, whether they're waiting at the grocery store, at a stop light, or for special friends to visit. Regardless of how hard it is, waiting is a fact of life — and it's often an important safety net to boot.

The sign for WAIT is a great communication tool for many occasions. For example, I use it daily when I'm trying to talk on the phone and my kids suddenly decide they need my undivided attention. Sound familiar? After many attempts, it actually works. Here's how to make the sign:

1. **With both hands, make the open-5 hand shape (see Chapter 3), palms facing up and fingertips curled.**

2. **Wiggle your fingers while making a stern face (see Figure 6-4).**

Figure 6-4: Now WAIT a minute!

Careful

CAREFUL is a fantastic sign to use with your baby and/or toddler. Think of it: From across the playground, you can tell your climber to be CAREFUL without yelling your head off. What a great idea, and it all starts with two simple steps:

1. Make two *K* hands (see Appendix A).

2. Turn your *K* hands sideways (pinkie-sides down), place one *K* hand on top of the other, and tap a few times (see Figure 6-5).

Figure 6-5: CAREFUL now!

Hurt

How many times a day does your precious bundle of joy get hurt? She falls down and bumps her head. She walks into the glass sliding door. She gets banged around by an older sibling. And don't forget when she gets her feelings hurt for one reason or another.

And on the other side of matters, what about when she head-butts you or explores with those tiny and strong teeth and jaw muscles? The bottom line: HURT is just a regular part of her (and your) day. You'll both get a lot of mileage out of this sign:

1. **Extend both index fingers and repeatedly almost touch their tips.**

   That action signs HURT in general. If you want to show a specific place on the body that HURTS, follow Step 2. If you want to show that *feelings* are HURT, skip Step 2 and follow Step 3 instead.

2. **If a specific body part hurts, move your hands to the vicinity of the body part that hurts while doing Step 1.**

   If your child's ear hurts, for example, make the HURT sign at your child's ear. If his knee hurts, make the sign there. Teeth? Sign at his mouth. And so on.

3. **If feelings are hurt instead of a body part, twist your hands and fingers in opposite directions over your heart while doing Step 1 and making a sad face (see Figure 6-6).**

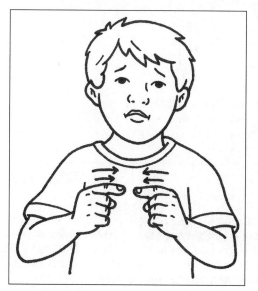

Figure 6-6: My feelings are HURT.

Help

As your baby has been growing and exploring, he has found that grunting tends to get him what he wants — until now. Any time during interactions with your baby, any moment when he needs you to do something for him, sign HELP. When the grunts and screams begin, say things like, "Do you want a cracker? Let Mommy HELP you." Then sign the word like this:

1. **Place a fist, thumb up, on top of the opposite palm.**

2. **While keeping that position, move both hands up (see Figure 6-7).**

   Imagine the palm hand helping the fist up.

Figure 6-7: Some HELP would be nice.

Sick

Next time your sweetheart throws up all over you or is miserable with a sinus infection, show her the sign for SICK to help her identify this yucky feeling. Take it from me, when your sweetie gets the hang of this sign, it'll be invaluable. Here's how to do it:

1. **Extend the middle fingers of both hands.**

2. **Place one finger in the middle of your forehead and the other at your belly button.**

3. **Tap your forehead and belly button a few times (see Figure 6-8).**

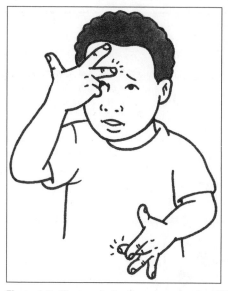

Figure 6-8: That yucky feeling means you're SICK.

Medicine

The sign for MEDICINE is great for use with teething-relief meds or even diaper-rash cream (see the nearby sidebar "Red-bottom blues"). And MEDICINE usually goes hand in hand with SICK or HURT. Explain to your little one what's going on ("I know your bottom is sore. I'll put some MEDICINE on it to make the HURT go away.") and simultaneously sign the pertinent words.

MEDICINE is signed like this:

1. **Extend the middle finger of one hand.**

2. **Cup the opposite hand and place the fingertip of your middle finger in its palm.**

3. **Move your middle finger around a few times without removing it from your palm (see Figure 6-9).**

   Think of your cupped hand as a mortar and your finger as a pestle from the days of grinding medicine.

Red-bottom blues

When my daughter Aidan Elizabeth was 16 months old, I was preparing to change her diaper one day, and as I pulled out the diaper and wipes, she looked up at me and signed MEDICINE and then patted her diaper. She hadn't been sick at all and I was confused.

"Aidan Elizabeth, why do you need MEDICINE?" I asked and signed. She repeated the sign and patted her diaper again. Still baffled, I went on with the diaper change. But as I wiped her bottom, I noticed the beginnings of a diaper rash. She needed diaper-rash cream for her reddening bottom, and she had figured out how to ask for it instead of just screaming to let me know she was in pain.

Figure 6-9: MEDICINE works wonders.

"How Do I Feel Today?" Signs

From screaming fits to fits of laughter, small children's mood swings can rival their parents' any day. Unfortunately, my kids are so tuned in to me that when I've had a bad day, they seem to have a bad day, too. Yikes. No pressure. Add those mood swings to 50,000 errands in the pouring rain and it's likely you who'll be pitching the fit. Identifying feelings for children as those feelings are expressed will help your kids be better communicators in the long run. And signing the feelings will enhance communication even more. Here are some feeling signs to get started.

Angry

Allowing children to be ANGRY in appropriate ways is crucial to their emotional development. Many people, myself included at times, allow anger to build up and then come out in one raging fit. Hmm, wonder if that's where my kids get it. . . .

Use the sign for ANGRY to help define a feeling exactly when your child is screaming and protesting something. For example, say, "You look ANGRY. I think you're ANGRY because your brother took your ball from you. It's all right to be ANGRY. Let's go tell brother you're ANGRY and ask to have your ball back."

Signing provides your little one a definition for his feelings, as well as reassures him that his feelings are perfectly normal. It's not the *feeling* that's the problem; it's what he *does* with the feeling that's important.

ANGRY takes over

A friend of mine was waiting in an airport with a frustrated toddler. Yikes. Luckily, this was also a signing toddler. In a last-ditch effort to entertain him, she allowed him to play in a nearby wheelchair that wasn't being used. Hey, whatever it takes to keep him happy, or just keep him from not screaming.

It was time to move on and Josh wasn't ready yet (surprise, surprise), so Beryt scooped him up and a walleyed fit ensued as she attempted to juggle her carry-on, the diaper bag and a screaming toddler. Oh yes, people were looking.

Having recently learned the sign for ANGRY, Beryt said, "Josh, are you ANGRY because Mommy took you away from the wheelchair? You're ANGRY because you still want to play with the wheelchair." Josh quit screaming, looked her in the eye, and signed ANGRY for the first time.

Here's how to make the ANGRY sign:

1. **Make the open-5 hand shape, palm toward your face (see Chapter 3).**

2. **Pull your hand away from your face, scrunching up your fingers (see Figure 6-10).**

   Your fingers represent the furrows that appear on an ANGRY face.

Figure 6-10: It's normal to feel ANGRY sometimes.

Happy

HAPPY was one of my son Cole's first words and signs. Of course, with Cole it sounds something like "appy" and the sign isn't exactly the way mine is, but it's still very cute to pick up Cole from a care-giver and watch him sign and say HAPPY. Trust me, this sign causes hearts to melt everywhere.

Now for the sign:

1. **Place your palms at upper-chest level, hands open and facing your torso.**

2. Make little circles with your hands or pat your chest (see Figure 6-11).

Think of your hands as your happy feelings when you peek at your sleeping baby. HAPPY just bubbles up out of your heart, which is fine unless it makes some noise and wakes up your sleeping angel.

Figure 6-11: If you're HAPPY and you know it, make the sign!

Sad

If you're around small children regularly (and I'm assuming you are — otherwise, why would you be reading this book?), you know that SAD is something that can happen at the drop of a hat, such as over hurt feelings or someone leaving. Get the sign SAD in your vocabulary and you can distract junior from a SAD fit or tantrum by giving him something to do with his hands:

1. Using both hands, place your spread-out fingers at your face, palms toward your head so that you're peeking out between your fingers.

2. Making a SAD face, draw your hands down to approximately shoulder level (see Figure 6-12).

This motion is emulating a child's drooping face. As you make the sign for SAD, imagine your child's face drooping when he isn't allowed something he desperately wants.

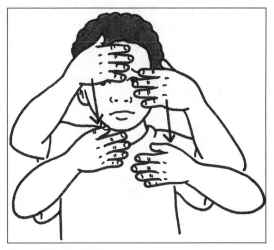

Figure 6-12: *So* SAD.

Scared

In Baby/Toddler World, feeling scared is common. Some children are scared of monsters in the middle of the night. Others are scared of the dark. And some are even scared of the loud bark of an unfamiliar dog. If feeling SCARED is part of your child's world, use the sign for SCARED to help her define the feeling: "I know you're SCARED, but I promise there are no monsters in your room. Look with me — no monsters under your bed or in your closet, so you don't have to feel SCARED anymore."

Here's how to make the sign:

1. **Make loose fists with both hands; place one at shoulder level, the other just above hip level.**

2. **While making a scared face, move your hands into the open-5 hand shape, wrists crossing each other quickly in front of your body as if you're protecting your body from something scary (see Figure 6-13).**

Figure 6-13: It's normal to feel SCARED sometimes.

Safe

SAFE is a great sign to use when you've just rescued your nervous baby from a boisterous older sibling or cousin. You can also use SAFE when baby is overwhelmed by his doting grandmother and needs the SAFETY of your arms. And if you're bonding with baby at his first baseball game, go ahead and excitedly sign, "And he's SAFE!" when a player steals home base, scoring for the home team. So many uses. Go for it:

1. **Cross your arms at your wrists, hands in S shapes, palms facing but not touching your body.**

2. **Pull your hands apart while twisting palms to face away from your body, stopping at the shoulder area. Keep those S shapes (see Figure 6-14).**

Figure 6-14: All SAFE now.

Sorry

It's bound to happen: At some point, your sweet little baby is going to do something that requires an apology. With any luck, the infraction will occur within the family unit and be as simple as, say, taking sister's toy. However, it may be something outside the family that draws blood, such as biting one of her friends during a play date. One way or another, your child needs to know that her action was wrong and that she must say she's sorry. If she's too young to talk yet, saying she's sorry through sign language is the way to go.

Here's the sign for SORRY:

1. **Make a sad, apologetic face.**

2. **Make an ASL letter *S* by forming a fist with your thumb wrapped around the outside of your fingers (see Appendix A).**

3. **Place your fist, palm facing your body, over your heart and make a circle (see Figure 6-15).**

   Remember your mom saying, "Apologies don't count unless they come from the heart."

Figure 6-15: From the heart, I'm truly SORRY.

TIP

Use the sign for SORRY in various situations where an apology is due so that your sweet little baby will begin to understand what SORRY really means. For example, say and sign, "Molly was reading that BOOK. Please give it back and tell her you're SORRY that you took it from her." Or say, "Bobby is HURT because you bit him. That made him CRY, and he needs MEDICINE to feel better. Tell Bobby you're SORRY for HURTing him." (The sign for BOOK is in Chapter 7; the signs for HURT, MEDICINE, and CRY are elsewhere in this chapter.)

Smile

Just like puppies, babies draw smiles wherever they go, assuming they're in a smiley mood, of course. A baby who's throwing a screaming fit in the checkout aisle *doesn't* draw smiles — that baby draws snarls.

Extra-cranky times aside, most babies do draw smiles from people they come into contact with. Of course, these are typically people who no longer have small children at home and are missing "the good ol' days." Believe me, sometimes I want to say, "Go ahead — take him and relive those days. . . . I could *really* use the break." But, alas, instead I usually say, "Yes, he's a doll. I wouldn't trade him for anything in the world." Except for a plane ticket to the Caribbean for a week. But I digress.

Help your baby define and understand the expression by showing him the sign for SMILE at various opportunities when others — or baby himself — is smiling. ***Bonus:*** Think of how you'll impress those lookey-loos if your smiley baby signs SMILE at an appropriate moment. Get ready, get set, SMILE:

1. **With both hands, form an ASL letter *L* by extending your index fingers and holding out your thumbs (see Appendix A).**

   In other words, form the shape of a capital *L* with your index finger and thumb — both hands here.

2. **Place the tips of your index fingers at the corners of your mouth and draw a SMILE up your cheeks, breaking into an actual smile while doing so (see Figure 6-16).**

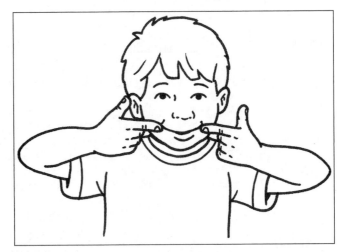

Figure 6-16: SMILE and the world smiles with you.

Laugh

Not much is more fulfilling than having a laughing child from a simple game of peek-a-boo. While you're both laughing in the midst of the game, be sure to sign LAUGH to help define the sound coming from his mouth and to help him understand the feeling associated with it. Say and sign something like, "This game is fun and it's making you LAUGH! It's making MAMA LAUGH, too!" Chapter 4 contains the sign for MAMA, and the following steps contain the sign for LAUGH:

1. **Make the sign for SMILE (see the preceding section for details).**

2. **Repeat the SMILE sign several times by continually drawing a smile on your face with your fingertips (see Figure 6-17).**

   Think of LAUGHING as expressing lots and lots of SMILES.

Figure 6-17: LAUGH till you cry — it's good for the soul.

Cry

Babies and crying go together like income and taxes. Can't have one without the other. As you know, babies cry because they're hurt, they're sleepy, they're hungry, they're bored, and simply because they're babies. They also tend to notice other children who are crying. On all such occasions, show your baby the sign for CRY to help her define the sound and understand the feeling associated with it. For example, the next time you see another child crying at the park, say and sign something like this: "That BABY fell down and is HURT — that's why he's CRYing." See Chapter 4 for BABY, Chapter 6 for HURT, and the following steps for the sign du jour, CRY:

1. **With both hands, extend your index fingers and touch them just under your eyes.**

2. **Pretend your fingers are tears and draw tracks of tears down your face (see Figure 6-18).**

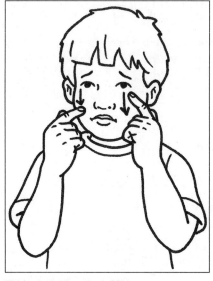

Figure 6-18: Aw, don't CRY.

Chapter 7

Bath and Bed Signs

- -

- -

*B*ath time and bedtime. For most adults, that sounds like heaven, especially after a long day of working hard and trying to keep up with the kids. But, as you're keenly aware, what sounds like heaven to adults is often, well, the opposite of heaven to kids. Granted, sometimes bath time and bedtime are a relaxing end to little sugar dumpling's busy day. But many times, sugar dumpling doesn't particularly like or want to cooperate with these two nightly routines, so he morphs into a sourpuss, turning the whole shebang into a nightmare of screaming, splashing water out of the tub, continuously waking up, and/or absolutely refusing to go to sleep. Lovely.

Signing to the rescue! This chapter covers a few basic signs to help you and your child communicate easily with each other from bath to bed — from dirty and disheveled to squeaky clean and snug as a bug in a rug. Now that *is* lovely.

Scrubbing in the Tub

The best time to introduce signs related to bath time isn't 10 a.m. at the kitchen table in a formal teaching lesson while junior's getting his midmorning fix of Cheerios and apple juice. Instead, you want to introduce bath-time signs in the natural context and setting of that particular routine in your house. For many people, that's in the early evening in the bathroom while junior's getting his *nightly* fix of being a sourpuss.

In this section, I cover four signs for communicating words that are common during scrub-a-dub-dub-in-the-tub time.

Bath

It's 7:30 p.m. on Monday night. Dinner's done, the jumbo building blocks are finally picked up and back in the toy box, and little buddy is rubbing his eyes. Perfect opportunity to introduce the sign for BATH. Catch your child's eye and say, "Almost time for BATH!" As you're saying BATH, sign the word like this:

1. **With both hands, make loose fists, thumbs on top.**

2. **Place your fists on your chest like you're Tarzan getting ready to beat on your chest.**

3. **Move your fists in several circles as if scrubbing your chest (see Figure 7-1).**

   You've just signed BATH. Piece of cake. (Well, not really. CAKE is in Chapter 5, which covers mealtime and various foods.)

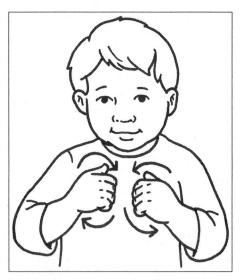

Figure 7-1: Signing the word BATH.

Always reinforce a sign by repeating yourself as often as possible after first introducing it. In the case of BATH, for example, after first introducing the sign, wait a minute and then do it again: Catch your child's eye a second time, say, "Let's go take a BATH!", and make the sign again very excitedly. Then scoop your child up and trot to the bathroom. Keep discussing and signing BATH throughout your bath-time routine.

Hey, Mom, I *really* need to get cleaned up!

When children are just 18 months old, parents generally don't expect them to say they're ready for the tub. In fact, 18-month-olds seem to want to stay dirty instead of washing up! But Aubrey was different. A signing baby, she liked to get squeaky clean after a full day of playing. On one particular day, after Aubrey finished with a pleasantly filthy experience in the mud, her mom asked if she was dirty. Aubrey laughed and signed BATH on the spot. She knew she was dirty and needed to get cleaned up. Aren't you ready for your child to tell you she's ready for her bath?

Water

Before depositing sweetie pie unceremoniously into the tub, better get the water going and test the temperature first. And why not sign the word WATER to keep her in the loop? Simply start the bath water and say, "Look! I'm putting WATER in the tub for your BATH!" Sign all the pertinent words as you say them. Here's how to sign the word du jour — WATER:

1. **Hold up three fingers, the sign for W (see Appendix A).**

2. **While still holding up your three fingers, tap your chin twice with the side of your first finger (see Figure 7-2).**

Figure 7-2: WATER, anyone?

After your child learns the sign for a word, she can sometimes use it in a totally different context. Take WATER, for example. When baby gets a handle on signing WATER, she can let you know that she's ready to get in the water for her bath or that she wants some water to drink. Same word, same sign, different uses.

American Sign Language doesn't have a sign for every word in the English language, and *tub* is one of those words without a specific sign. So you have to work around the issue by using a combo of other signs to get the point across. For purposes of this book, though, if you have BATH and WATER covered, you're in good shape during bath time with baby, so don't fret about trying to come up with a combination of signs for *tub*.

Bubbles

Water and bubbles go together like peas and carrots. If you have a young'un in the house, chances are you also have a bottle of bubble bath in the cabinet. So why not take an opportunity to let your little one communicate an independent decision? Show him how to sign BUBBLES and regularly ask him, "Do you want some BUBBLES in your BATH?" Here's how to make the sign:

1. **Make the flat-O hand shape with both hands, fingertips pointing up (see Chapter 3).**

2. **Open and close your hands while alternately moving them up and down in front of your body (see Figure 7-3).**

The signs for PLAY and STOP can come in handy when communicating info about bubbles in the tub. (Ditto when communicating info about splashing in the tub, covered in the following section.) If you're interested in finding out how to sign PLAY, turn to Chapter 10. And for STOP, turn to Chapter 6.

Splash

Little ones are notorious for making messes during bath time. After all, splashing water is loads of fun — and so is splashing Mom and Dad. For a kid, watching your reaction to getting a little bit wet is totally worth bearing your wrath afterward.

Figure 7-3: Yay! BUBBLES!

As with many things in life, moderation is key. So is communication. Develop both with your little one by using the sign for SPLASH during bath time:

1. **Make two fists and place them together in front of your body.**

2. **In a quick movement, move your fists out to the opposite sides of your body, showing the number five (see Appendix B) with both hands, palms facing away from your body (see Figure 7-4).**

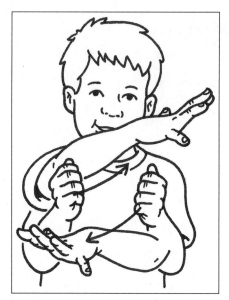

Figure 7-4: SPLASH!

Getting Ready for Bed

So your little bundle of energy is done with her bath and clean as a whistle, and now you're ready to wind her down and send her gently into la-la land. Using a simple signing routine at bedtime each night will help develop solid communication between you and your child, and the consistency aspect will help your child feel in the know and more secure during bedtime.

This section covers signs for a few words that are commonly used during bedtime routines. If your child's routine is currently a nightmare, incorporating these two-way-communication signs may help turn the nightmare into a dream.

Toothbrush

Time to get those pearly whites sparkling! Although babies generally do little more than chew on their toothbrushes, TOOTHBRUSH is still a useful sign:

1. **Extend your index finger on either hand.**

2. **Pretending your index finger is a toothbrush, place it parallel with your mouth.**

3. **Open your lips, show your teeth, and move your index finger up and down (see Figure 7-5).**

    Feel free to add sound effects to mimic the sound of a toothbrush brushing while signing. Even if you feel a bit goofy, your baby will likely pay more attention because you're making an odd sound!

Figure 7-5: Brushing with my TOOTHBRUSH.

Tired

Whether it's you or your sweetie pie, feeling exhausted is common in families with small children. Using a sign to communicate this reality is helpful, and the sign TIRED does the job just fine.

1. **Place the fingertips of both hands on the front of each respective shoulder.**

    You may look a bit like a duck flapping its wings. (If this stance has put you in a ducky mood, feel free to discover the sign for DUCK in Chapter 9 on animals.)

2. **Roll your shoulders in, letting your hands move with them (see Figure 7-6).**

    Imagine (probably not too difficult right now) that you're so exhausted, you can't even hold your shoulders back. (Sorry about the bad posture, Mom!)

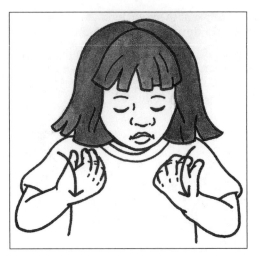

Figure 7-6: Slumpy me, I'm *so* TIRED.

American Sign Language is a very expressive language. Make sure your facial expression matches whatever sign you're trying to communicate with your baby (or anyone else for that matter).

Bed

When you or your sweetie pie is TIRED, hopefully you can go to BED. If you're lucky, this scenario may actually happen at the same time. Be ready to communicate with the sign for BED:

1. **Place the palm of your hand on your ear.**

   If you use your left hand, use your left ear. If you use your right hand, use your right ear.

2. **Tilt your head to the same side, as if you're using your hand for a pillow (see Figure 7-7).**

Figure 7-7: Careful, don't fall asleep while signing BED.

Sleep

Granted, I realize full well that sleep can be elusive with a baby or toddler in the house. I have three toddlers in my house, so I'm all too familiar with this concept. Regardless of the odds against you, don't give up on the quest for sleep. At naptime and bedtime, always say and sign the magic words. Reiterate to sweetie pie that you know he's TIRED, which is why he's in BED. Then say, "It's time for you to SLEEP now," and sign the word like this:

1. **Using an open-5 hand shape, have your palm looking at your face (see Chapter 3).**

2. **Slowly pull the open-5 hand shape into a flat-O hand shape (again, see Chapter 3), fingertips up.**

3. **As you pull your open-5 hand into a flat-O, roll your head forward (see Figure 7-8).**

    Your head is so heavy you can't hold it up anymore!

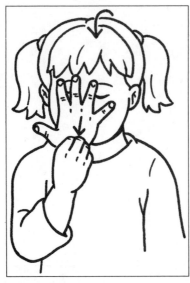

Figure 7-8: SLEEP, baby, SLEEP. *Please.*

Book

Okay, so sweetie pie is acting more like a grapefruit (sour). She's tired, she's in bed, but she's certainly not willing to go to sleep just yet. Reading can be a calming transition to nighty-night time, and the sign for BOOK can also be useful when she pulls all the books off the shelf, leaving a terrific mess that needs to be cleaned up. Coax little grapefruit back into a sweetie pie (à la) mode by saying, "We'll read a BOOK if you'll go to SLEEP as soon as we're done."

Here's how to sign the magic word BOOK:

1. **Place your palms together in front of your body, finger-tips pointing away from your body.**

2. **Open your hands, palms facing up, like you're opening a book (see Figure 7-9).**

When reading with your child, pick out one or two signs to sign throughout the book. What does the book have on every page? If it's a DOG, sign DOG every time you turn the page. (DOG and more animal signs are covered in Chapter 9.) And don't forget the always-there, handy-dandy sign for WHAT (see Chapter 1). The sign for WHAT can get you through any book, in addition to just about any other situation with your little sweetie.

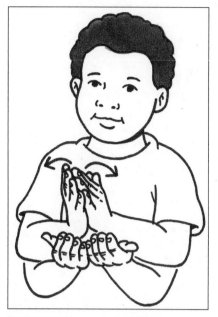

Figure 7-9: Wanna read a BOOK?

Bear

Whether it's a teddy BEAR, monkey, or doll, children usually have some type of lovey to hold onto at night. You know, the one you're always retrieving in the middle of the night after it falls out of the bed (or, worse, running out to the family car in your jammies to fetch before your little one can calm down and go to sleep). I'm giving you the sign for BEAR because it's one of the most common companions, but you can look up some other animals in Chapter 9 if you need them:

1. **Make an *X* with your arms over your chest, palms near shoulders.**

2. **Use your fingertips and nails to scratch your chest a couple of times (see Figure 7-10).**

   Growl a bit for some added fun!

Figure 7-10: Who needs his teddy BEAR?

Blanket

Sometimes sweetie may be thinking, "Forget the teddy, I want my blankey!" And because sweetie can't say the words yet, the sign for BLANKET comes in very handy:

1. **Make loose fists, palms facing the floor at your waist.**

2. **Pull your hands up to shoulder level like you're pulling up a warm and cuddly BLANKEY (see Figure 7-11).**

Lights

At some point in your child's evening routine, the time for LIGHTS out in one form or fashion will finally and mercifully come. Hallelujah! Hopefully, your little sweetie is nodding off enough to avoid any screaming. Here's how to sign that it's time for LIGHTS out:

1. **Using a flat-O hand shape, raise your hand above your head with fingertips pointing down.**

2. **Spread your fingers out to create an open-5 hand shape (see Chapter 3) to show that the lights are currently on.**

3. **Pull your fingers back into the flat-O hand shape to show that it's time for LIGHTS to go out (see Figure 7-12).**

Figure 7-11: Gimme my BLANKEY, please.

Figure 7-12: LIGHTS out!

Whew! Now that sweetie is drifting off into dreamland, take a break . . . and hurry to get some shuteye yourself before you're awakened in a few hours to find the bear or blankey that's hit the floor.

Part III

Signs for Everyday Life

The 5th Wave   By Rich Tennant

"Oh, now that's a new sign I don't recognize."

In this part . . .

So tell me, what makes baby go ga-ga? Is it animals? Trains? The wind blowing in his face? Baby is more likely to respond to signs for items he's interested in. Although interests vary from baby to baby, there are a few commonly agreed upon objects of affection, and they're usually things that are part of baby's everyday life.

That's the focus of Part III — signs for everyday life. Here, you find signs for clothing (don't you love how they empty out the sock drawer when you're not looking?), signs for some popular animals (including some of my family's favorites), and signs for objects in the great outdoors. What are a few of your baby's favorite things? Go ahead, sing the song and get signing.

Chapter 8

Signing Stuff That Baby Wears

In This Chapter

▶ Getting dressed with signs

▶ Signing clothes to keep baby warm

*W*hat to wear, what to wear. My three kids have more clothes in their closets than I do. Really. They were the first grand-kids on both sides of the family, and seven grandparents and three great-grandmothers have supplied more clothes than we'll ever know what to do with. Keeping up with all those clothes is a night-mare. The girls' sock drawer alone strikes fear in my heart with all the colors, beads, and lace. Think about the maintenance. I mean, who really wants or has time to iron or line-dry all those items loaded with assorted frou-frou?

If you're like me, you'll realize soon enough that buying the basics is much easier and much more cost-effective than buying fancy outfits. Besides, let's be frank: The moment she's dressed in that gorgeous smocked dress that cost you (or your mother) major bucks, Little Miss Messy Mess poops or spits up or spills all over it. And then there's the quick strip and soak in an attempt to get the stain out. Ack.

In this chapter, I give you some signs for *basic* clothing. Trust me, basic is the best way to go — with clothing as well as signs for baby.

Typical Playwear

Playing is a major part of the day for babies and toddlers. And to make the most of their day, they need to be wearing clothing that doesn't get in the way. I'm talking about everyday wear, rough-and-tumble clothes, your basic shirt, pants, socks, and shoes. In this section, I cover the signs for these very items. When you're getting baby dressed in the morning, start talking about how he's going to PLAY today (you can find the sign for PLAY in Chapter 10) and discuss each item of clothing as you put it on him.

Shirt

One of my daughter Darby's biggest milestones to date was learning to take her SHIRT off by herself. She'd say, "Watch me!" and take off her SHIRT. Then we'd have to clap. Ah, firstborn children. . . .

A good time to introduce signs to babies is when you're showing them how to do various tasks, like putting on or taking off their shirt. So anytime you're putting on or taking off your baby's shirt, say and sign the word. In addition, use the sign for SHIRT when you have a fussy baby who's refusing to get dressed. With any luck, signing will distract her long enough for you to slip the SHIRT over her head. And if all else fails, there's always the peek-a-boo game with the SHIRT. Usually, playing peek-a-boo turns babies from fussy to fascinated lickety-split.

Here's the SHIRT sign:

1. **With the index finger and thumb of each hand, pinch a bit of your shirt just below your shoulders.**

2. **Pull out and let go of the shirt a couple of times (see Figure 8-1).**

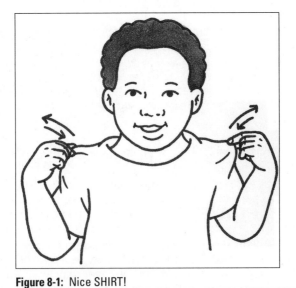

Figure 8-1: Nice SHIRT!

Pants

Recently, my son Cole discovered the fasteners on his diapers. Then he started taking his diaper off and running around the house naked, which inevitably led to him peeing somewhere. Last week, it was on my foot. The girls never did anything like this.

I have a point here. The way my husband and I have discovered to combat this act of nudity (and the bodily function that always accompanies it) is fairly simple: We leave PANTS on him all the time. He hasn't yet figured out how to pull down the PANTS and get to the diaper. Yes, I know the day will come, but for now PANTS seem to do the trick.

If you have a budding nudist as well, try using this strategy to keep your own feet dry. And while putting pants on He Who Streaks A Lot, go ahead and communicate what you're doing: "Here are your PANTS! Let's put your PANTS on before you go PLAY!" See Chapter 10 for the PLAY sign and see the following steps for the PANTS sign:

1. **Face your palms toward each other, about 6 inches apart, fingertips pointing down.**

2. **Starting at your waist, move both hands down one leg, back up to your waist, and then down your other leg (see Figure 8-2).**

Socks

Don't get me started on baby socks. Granted, they're *so* tiny and they come in such wonderful coordinating colors and cute little prints. But take warning here: They seem to multiply on their own. Nearly every baby outfit has matching socks to go with it, and as a result, my daughters' sock drawer is overflowing.

The upside is that baby socks, even the frou-frou kind, serve a functional purpose — to keep those little piggy toes warm — so you'll get good use out of them. When you're shuffling through the sock drawer in the morning, trying to find the pair that matches the outfit du jour, sign away to show baby what you're looking for. She'll get the hang of the sign soon enough, and then one day when you're running late and need to cover her feet, she can help you find the SOCKS she shed during breakfast, playtime, or in the car.

Figure 8-2: PANTS: Never leave home without 'em.

Here's the sign:

1. **Extend both index fingers and place them, touching, side by side, fingertips pointing down.**

2. **While keeping your fingers touching, alternate moving them up and down, pointing toward your socks, repeating the motion several times (see Figure 8-3).**

Figure 8-3: SOCKS make piggy toes happy.

Shoes

Shoes are big business. Everybody knows that. But did you know *baby* shoes are big business? You can buy nearly any brand of adult shoes in baby sizes and pay almost as much as you do for your own shoes. This is especially true in the athletic-shoe market. (No surprise there, eh?)

No matter what kind you choose to put on your baby's feet, or whether they're for function or show, the sign for SHOES is the same:

1. **Make two fists, thumbs in front.**

2. **Tap your fists together a couple of times (see Figure 8-4).**

   Why the tapping? Think of Dorothy in *The Wizard of Oz* click-click-clicking her heels together. Little dog optional.

Figure 8-4: Love your SHOES!

Stuff That Keeps Baby Toasty Outside

Depending on where you live, the weather outside can be frightful. And sometimes you just can't stay inside, where it's so delightful. So if there's someplace to go, you gotta deal with the snow, with the snow, with the snow. Or something like that.

During such times, your baby may not understand all the extra-thick clothing you throw on her or the strange feeling that envelops her when she steps outside (the brrrr feeling), but both are a part of life. Use sign language to help her understand what all the fuss is about. This section gives you the signs for three basic pieces of outerwear that keep babies toasty and comfortable: HAT, COAT, and MITTENS.

Hat

Hats are an important piece of outerwear when you're heading outside. They trap body heat to help keep you warm. The bonus is
that even if you're not heading outside, hats can still be an important piece of outerwear. Hats are fun to play with, and at my house,
we have tons of dress-up HATS for just about every occupation,
from princess to firefighter. As a result, the sign for HAT is a favorite
of my kids. They even use the sign HAT for a family friend who
wears a HAT regularly.

The sign is the same no matter what the occasion. Next time you're
off to play in any weather, inside or out, use the sign HAT when it's
time to put one on your baby's head:

1. **Make a flat hand with one hand.**

2. **Pat your head a few times (see Figure 8-5).**

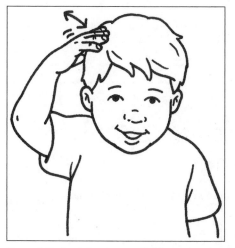

Figure 8-5: Don't forget your HAT!

Coat

I live in southeast Texas, so we don't get much chance to use
heavy winter coats. My family owns them, but last winter we only
pulled them out once, when the high was 34°F (1°C) and it was

raining and icy. School was cancelled that day. The next day the high was 72°F (22°C), and by the end of the week we were wearing shorts. Such is life in southeast Texas.

Whether it's a big, thick snow coat or a windbreaker or a raincoat, a COAT comes in handy in many types of weather, in Texas as well as other parts of the country. Be ready no matter what the forecast with the sign for COAT:

1. **Make two fists and place them by each shoulder like you're about to lift weights.**

2. **Pull both fists in to meet in the center of your chest, as if you're pulling on a coat (see Figure 8-6).**

Figure 8-6: It's freezing out there, so put your COAT on!

Mittens or gloves

A couple of years ago, my husband and I had a snow-themed birthday party for one of the kids. We had a great time playing with the snow, which — because we live in Texas — we created out of packing peanuts and tossed into a kiddie pool. In addition, we created snow pictures and tried on GLOVES. Because of the climate in Texas, my girls didn't remember ever wearing GLOVES before, and they were fascinated with the discount-store variety we gave out as favors.

For those of you who, like me, live in warmer climates, I highly recommend snow-themed birthday parties for a change of pace, with
MITTENS or GLOVES as unique party favors. And then there's
everyone else — those of you who actually *live* in colder climates.
Personally, I don't know how you make it through the winter, but I
do know that *you* know the importance of MITTENS or GLOVES to
protect those tiny little fingers from the cold. So whether for play
or for real, when MITTENS or GLOVES are in the picture, communicate to your child what they are by using this sign:

1. **Place one hand, palm down, fingers spread, in front
   of you.**

2. **Place your other hand, palm down, fingers spread, on top
   of your first hand.**

3. **Pull your top hand back as if you're pulling on MITTENS
   or GLOVES and then switch hands (see Figure 8-7).**

   Note: You can use this sign interchangeably for MITTENS
   and GLOVES.

Figure 8-7: MITTENS or GLOVES are a must when it's cold outside.

Chapter 9

Signing Animals from A to Z

In This Chapter

▶ Knowing the signs for your family pets

▶ Showing your little one the signs for farm animals

▶ Making your next trip to the zoo even more fun with signs

*A*nimals are a big deal for babies and toddlers. Maybe the reason is because, unlike most things in kids' lives, many animals are actually smaller than the kids are. Or maybe it's because animals make strange and different noises, much like kids themselves. Kids see animals in books, on videos, and even in their nursery décor. Maybe that's where the love comes from. Who knows? For that matter, who cares? The source of the interest isn't the point. What you can *do* with the interest is what matters.

The subject of animals presents a huge opportunity for two-way communication between baby and you, so this chapter covers a few signs for three different groups of common animals: pets, farm animals, and zoo animals. I focus on common animals kids see in a variety of settings.

Can We Have a Pet? Please, Please, Please?

My daughter Aidan Elizabeth has always been fascinated with animals. Her parents, however, have *not* had the energy to take in any animals — three babies in less than three years zaps your energy pretty quickly — so Aidan Elizabeth has been without a family pet all her life. Until recently. For her third birthday, a set of her grandparents gave her an aquarium. She was *so* excited. So much so that her aquarium might even be considered the best gift she's ever received in her short life.

Needless to say, however, less than two weeks after receiving said best gift she's ever received in her short life, we were down four fish and had to take them back to the pet store in a plastic bag. Gotta love those life lessons. And speaking of life lessons, one of our fish recently gave birth — to 30 fish. Yes, 30. Not a single one has had to be flushed, so I guess we're making up for the returned ones.

But I digress. You'll find out sooner rather than later, if you haven't found out already, that pets are going to be a *huge* topic in your household. To help you discuss the topic with your child, this section covers signs for some common household pets. If you already own one of these pets, use the sign whenever it's around. And if you and little dumpling are looking at a book that has one of these animals on every page, sign away. Remember to have fun with this topic because it's, well, simply the cat's meow to kids.

Dog

My daughter Aidan Elizabeth, proud new owner of her very own aquarium and pet fish, isn't the only animal lover in the house. My son, Cole, loves animals just as much, and DOGS are his favorite. We don't own a DOG, but every time Cole hears a DOG or sees a DOG, he signs DOG and even attempts a little bark.

When you're making the sign for an animal, go ahead and add the sound the animal makes. Doing so gets your child's attention, adds auditory stimulation, and teaches him the sound that goes with the animal. Plus, it's big fun, so live a little.

My advice is to follow Cole's example: Whenever you hear a dog or see a dog, say the word and sign away — and attempt a little bark yourself. "Look! There's Bobby and his DOG. Woof, woof! See the DOG? Woof! What a pretty DOG!" Here's the sign:

1. **Tap your leg with an open hand.**

2. **After the tap, lift your hand and snap one time (see Figure 9-1).**

   Rather intuitive, wouldn't you say? I mean, what do you do to get a dog to come to you? Many times you snap your fingers. You'll find that lots of ASL signs are intuitive, which makes them easier to remember.

Figure 9-1: DOG-gone cute!

Cat

Like dogs, cats are popular family pets. Even if your family doesn't have one, chances are an immediate family member or close friend does. When you and junior are around kitty cats, be ready to discuss them with the sign for CAT:

1. **Pinch your index finger and thumb together in the ASL sign for *F* (see Appendix A), leaving the rest of your fingers spread apart.**

2. **Touch the center of your cheek with you pinched fingers and stroke toward your ear a few times (see Figure 9-2).**

   Pretend you're stroking whiskers on a cat.

Figure 9-2: Look, a CAT! Here kitty, kitty.

Fish

It doesn't matter where you go, you run into aquariums just about everywhere. Our family doctor's office has two of them. Our favorite restaurant has three. And, of course, there's Daughter Dear's aquarium at our house.

I can think of many reasons aquariums are so popular. Out in the real world — for example, in a doctor's office or restaurant — think of how useful they are when you're trying to distract a waiting child. While showing Fidgety Britches all the interesting stuff in the tank, say and sign the word FISH frequently. Here's the sign:

1. **Extend your hand as if you're about to shake hands.**

2. **Wiggle your hand from side to side (see Figure 9-3) while moving it forward.**

   Pretend your wiggling hand is a fish swimming in water.

Figure 9-3: FISH wish.

Bird

Before our son was born, my husband and I took our girls, Darby and Aidan Elizabeth, to an indoor rainforest. One of the attractions was a bright blue parrot that could squawk a blue streak (sorry, couldn't resist). The girls came upon the parrot, and Aidan Elizabeth turned around and signed BIRD to her father and me. About that time, the parrot began squawking and the girls erupted into huge fits of giggles. What a fun way to spend the afternoon! We found out firsthand that birds are great entertainment.

If you look outside your window or go outside to play, you're bound to see some type of BIRD to point out to your child. Or maybe there's a BIRD on a video she watches. Or, if you have a difficult time finding BIRDS in your everyday life, go to a pet store and check out the display there. Who knows? You may come home with a family pet.

Regardless of where you find them, the goal is to talk them up while signing away (and simultaneously chirping or squawking). The sign for BIRD goes like this:

1. **Make a fist and extend your index finger and thumb.**

2. **Place the back of your hand to your chin.**

3. **Open and close your index finger and thumb (see Figure 9-4).**

   Yep, your fingers are representing the beak of a BIRD.

Figure 9-4: BIRDS of a feather . . .

Look Down Thar by the Barn and Pasture

I used to be a first-grade teacher, and I once had an entire class of kids who grew up on concrete. The only exposure to animals most of them ever got were the stray dogs and cats that hung around their apartments.

As luck would have it, one of the class fieldtrips that year was to a farm a couple of hours away from the school. What a treat it was for me to watch those 6- and 7-year-olds experience animals and a farm for the very first time! They rode horses, milked cows, and fed goats. We had a great time, and I'm sure most of those kids still have memories as vivid as the ones I have about that special day.

Even if your view from home is concrete in all directions and your baby has never crawled outside the city limits, chances are that he's still been exposed to lots of information about farms and farm animals, from e-i-e-i-o songs to books about various critters that live way out by the barn and pasture. You can enhance your child's understanding of these critters by using the signs for them during your conversations. This section starts you on your way with signs for some basic farm animals: cow, horse, sheep, pig, chicken, duck, and frog.

 If you're lucky enough to have a farm within driving distance, and if that farm allows visitors (especially visitors with babies in tow), why not get a group of friends together to make the trip? The pictures alone will be worth the effort. You'll be able to introduce your baby firsthand to various farm animals, as well as show the signs for the animals on the spot. Then, when you get back home, you'll be able to reminisce and reinforce the learning experience by looking at the photos and continuing with the signs.

Cow

Moo. Babies see COWS on ice cream and milk cartons, in animal books, and even in fast-food restaurants occasionally. Recently, for example, during a grand reopening of a popular chicken sandwich chain in my neck of the woods, my kids were given stuffed COWS to commemorate the occasion. Being the signing big sisters that they are, the girls immediately began getting brother Cole's attention by mooing and signing COW. Cole just laughed and laughed and finally attempted the sign and the moo, much to the girls' (and their parents') delight.

Next time you see a COW, whether in a pasture or barn, on a carton or billboard, in a book or picture, feel free to re-create my family's experience at the fast-food restaurant. That is, if you don't think you'd feel a little out of place mooing and signing in public. Here's the sign for COW:

1. **Make the ASL sign for the letter Y by making a fist and then extending your thumb and pinkie finger (see Appendix A).**

2. **Place your thumb to your temple (see Figure 9-5).**

   Picture a bull's horn. (For those of you who may have grown up on concrete, a bull is a male cow.) Now you've got it.

Figure 9-5: Got COWS?

Horse

Whether they have majestic wings, a magical horn, or a shimmering knight on top, horses in many storybooks are the source of happily-ever-after dreams of children everywhere. And then there's the other side of the saddle. I'm talking about the farming, sporting, ranching, herding, rodeoing, ten-gallon-hat-and-chaps-wearing, horse-loving children, and there are lots of them, too. I'm from Texas. I should know.

Whether your little horse lover is into fairytales or farms, ranches or rodeos, have fun with your imaginations, books, and fieldtrips — and sign the word HORSE all the while. Here's how:

1. **Make a fist and then extend your first two fingers and thumb, fingertips pointing up.**

2. **Place your thumb on your head above your ear and bend your fingers forward a couple of times (see Figure 9-6).**

   Yep, you're pretending your fingers are a horse's ears.

Figure 9-6: Giddy up, HORSE.

Sheep

Baa, baa, black SHEEP. My kids and I were singing this song recently when Darby asked, "Mommy, what's a SHEEP?" She knew the sign for SHEEP and the sound a SHEEP makes, but she had no clue what a SHEEP was. So I pulled out books and did some quick online research to find pictures of SHEEP so my kids could put a picture with the word and sound. Isn't it funny how we assume kids know things?

To avoid this situation with your baby, show him pictures of SHEEP and other animals when singing about them, talking about them, and making their various sounds. And all the while, show him the sign too. Here's how to make the sign for SHEEP:

1. **Extend a bent arm in front of you.**

2. **Use the first two fingers of your other hand to create "scissors."**

3. **Move your "scissors" up and down the other arm (see Figure 9-7).**

   This action mimics shearing a sheep.

Figure 9-7: Baa, baa, black SHEEP.

Pig

Whether it's Piglet, devoted friend of Winnie the Pooh, or Big Mama and her babies, mud-wallowing oinkers on Grandpa Kettle's farm, PIGS hold a fascination for young babies and toddlers. Piglet is fascinating thanks to the magic of great storytelling. Real pigs are fascinating for quite a different reason. Just think about it from a toddler's standpoint: A PIG is a being that grunts, plays in the mud, enjoys it, and doesn't get in trouble for it. I sure don't blame little sweetie-peeties for staring at PIGS or for idolizing them if they so desire.

So the next time you see your little one staring at a PIG, excitedly share in her joy. Say something like "Wow! Look at that big PIG! The PIG is playing in the mud! What a funny PIG!" and show her the sign each time you said the magic word. Go ahead and add an oink if you're game — your baby will love it.

Here's the sign:

1. **Make the ASL sign for *B* by holding all four fingers of one hand straight up, touching, while laying your thumb against your palm (see Appendix A).**

2. **Place the top of your letter *B* hand under your chin.**

3. **Bend your fingers down once or twice (see Figure 9-8).**

   Ever heard the saying "You eat like a pig!" Your fingers are representing a pig eating his slop (or sloppily eating, if you prefer). I know — ewwww.

Figure 9-8: Signing PIG.

Chicken

So my oldest daughter, Darby, knew the sign for CHICKEN from seeing various chickens at several petting zoos and on a farm trip. That's fine and dandy, yes, but one night we were *eating* CHICKEN for dinner and my husband signed CHICKEN to our son, Cole. Darby said, "Daddy, that's not the sign for eating CHICKEN. That's the sign for CHICKENS that walk around." Uh-oh. Awkward parenting moment. Carefully, I hope, we explained to our 3-year-old how the signs were the same and why they were the same.

I've said it before, and I know I'll say it again and again during this long journey as a parent: Gotta love those life lessons. It's actually a wonder any of us ever ate CHICKEN again.

Hopefully, your baby's introduction to the multiuse sign for CHICKEN won't be quite so traumatic, for him or for you. When you're ready, here's the sign for CHICKEN. Cluck it up:

1. **Cup one hand in front of your body, palm facing up.**

2. **Make the sign for BIRD with your other hand.**

3. **Move your extended fingers to the center of your other palm and tap your hand a few times (see Figure 9-9).**

    The movement is reminiscent of a CHICKEN pecking the ground.

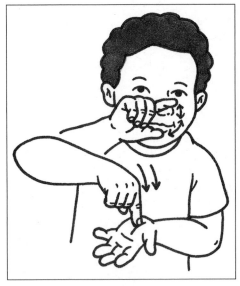

Figure 9-9: Eat more CHICKEN.

Duck

I know, I know. You can see DUCKS at your local park and at the zoo, not just down on the farm. In fact, one of my family's favorite pastimes is feeding the DUCKS at a nearby pond. That pond is where my husband and I went to show our kids what DUCKS really are — not just vague beings from funny songs or floating plastic bath toys. It's also where Aidan Elizabeth signed DUCK for the first time (also one of her first words, by the way). I guess it's safe to say ducks are a pretty big deal at my house.

Whatever your occasion — whether feeding live ducks at the farm/park/pond/zoo or singing a ducky song, reading a ducky book, or playing with a rubber ducky in the bath (the sign for BATH is in Chapter 7, by the way) — use the occasion to introduce the sign, have a good time, and add a "quack, quack" for good measure.

Here's the sign for DUCK:

1. **Make the sign for BIRD (refer to Figure 9-4, earlier in this chapter.)**

2. **Add your middle finger beside your index finger (see Figure 9-10).**

   The movement imitates a duck's bill.

Figure 9-10: Rubber DUCKY, you're the one.

Frog

Last summer, several FROGS decided to camp out by my back door. I don't know why. Of course, Aidan Elizabeth was fascinated and wanted to follow them around. One night, we brought a flashlight outside and followed a FROG around the patio, signing FROG the whole time. When the FROG hopped off into the yard (no doubt to get away from the shrieks of glee), Aidan Elizabeth followed it, bare feet and all, shouting, "Come back FROGGY! I love you!" She signed and yelled those words over and over again as her father and I keeled over from laughter. It's a memory we'll never forget.

Hopefully, you and your little one will have an opportunity to see and chase live FROGS sometime, but even if Kermit ends up being the only FROG your baby gets exposed to, use said Muppet as an opportunity to introduce the sign for FROG. Here it is:

1. **Place a fist under your chin.**

2. **Move your first two fingers out and in several times, with your thumb catching the fingers on the in movement (see Figure 9-11).**

   The movement is mimicking a bullFROG's chin area blowing up as it makes its sound.

Figure 9-11: FROGGIE tales.

Fieldtrip! A Day at the Zoo

A day at the zoo can be fantastic fun for all involved, if you're up to walking your legs off and stepping through a smelly area or two. I say this from direct experience. Last summer on a bright, sunshiny day in May, my best friend and her daughter, my girls, my mother, and I headed out for the local zoo. We walked and walked and walked. The first thing my girls saw were some stuffed monkeys at a shop, and they immediately jumped out of the wagon to go play with them. I headed toward the shop to deposit the girls straight back in the wagon, but my mom beat me there and started to play with the girls and the monkeys. Great. Like we needed more stuffed animals at our house. But being the Master Mother she is, my mom actually coaxed the girls away from the shop without purchasing a monkey and without a screaming fit from either child. I view this as nothing short of a miracle.

Of course, we went directly to the monkey area (smelly area #1) where the girls enjoyed acting like monkeys the whole time. They signed MONKEY and made monkey noises through the rest of the zoo. At the elephant area (smelly area #2), they signed ELEPHANT, trumpeted, and then went back to being monkeys. At the lion's den (interestingly, smelly area not so much), they signed LION and roared a bit, and then went back to being monkeys. Same thing when we saw the tigers, bears, and alligators. Yet we still didn't go home with a stuffed monkey. Go figure.

Next time you take your bundle of love to the zoo, have a few animal signs in your back pocket. The signs will help keep your kids (and others) entertained throughout the whole zoo trip. This section can get you started by providing signs for a few common zoo animals.

Monkey

My family recently went to a monkey-themed birthday party. We had bananas with a monkey-shaped cake. Too cute. The party favor was a 2-foot-tall blow-up monkey. We brought home three of them. My daughters buckled their monkeys into the spare car seat in our van. Son Cole just wouldn't let go of his monkey. When we got home, the monkeys disappeared into the toy room until the next morning. Cole found his monkey and started carrying it around, holding it by the hand. The next time I saw him, Cole had his arms around the monkey and was giving it hugs and kisses. Aren't kids hilarious?

Next time you're around a monkey — real or toy — make a big deal of the situation by pretending you're a monkey, jumping around and making monkey noises. Of course, this activity may be better suited for you dads out there, to whom it may come a bit more naturally. Whichever of you is willing to embarrass yourself in front of other people is the best one to demonstrate, but don't forget to make the sign for MONKEY while you do it:

1. **Place the fingertips of both hands at your waist.**

2. **Move your fingertips up to your armpits.**

3. **Repeat several times (see Figure 9-12).**

Figure 9-12: Let's MONKEY around, baby.

Lion

There's nothing more royal than a lion perched on a rock looking disinterested in everything around it. Sort of like your baby when he's not interested in shopping but can't find a reason to fuss about it yet. When you're around lions next time, show your sweetie pie the sign for LION while making a big roar. It's guaranteed to get his attention.

Here's the sign for LION:

1. **Rest your hand on top of your head with your fingertips facing forward at your forehead.**

2. **Pull your hand back and down to the back of your neck (see Figure 9-13).**

   Your hand is representing a lion's mane as you make this sign.

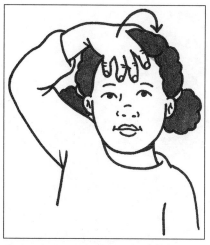

Figure 9-13: Roar, LION, roar.

Tiger

Tigers always seem restless to me. Every time I see tigers, they seem to be impatiently walking around whatever habitat they're in, sort of the way my husband paced while I was in labor.

Anyway, next time you glimpse a tiger pacing at the zoo, or watch a video of Tigger bouncing through the Hundred Acre Wood, have fun with the TIGER sign. ***Bonus:*** It's also great for a game of peek-a-boo.

1. **Open your fingers and loosely lace them together, palms facing your body.**

2. **Place your loosely laced fingers at your nose.**

3. **Pull your hands apart, toward your ears (see Figure 9-14).**

   Your hands are representing stripes on a tiger's face.

Elephant

Elephants hold massive fascination for most people, especially if you're under 3 feet tall and drink from a sippy cup. ELEPHANT was one of my daughter Aidan Elizabeth's first signs. Her aunt and uncle gave her a stuffed elephant, which she loved immensely and took everywhere we went.

Figure 9-14: TIGER, raah!

Whether your child's first experience is with a real elephant or a stuffed one, the sign is the same. Don't forget to make a trumpeting sound as you're making the sign:

1. **Place the back of your hand at your nose and mouth area.**

2. **Move your hand out and up, like you're outlining an elephant's trunk (see Figure 9-15).**

Figure 9-15: ELEPHANT, schmelephant.

Alligator

As parents, we sing about alligators, read about alligators, and see them at the zoo. We even take care of our own little alligators during teething and biting times. During any and all of these activities, take the time to say and sign ALLIGATOR to keep your baby in the know. (By the way, you can use the same sign for ALLIGATOR and CROCODILE.)

Here's the sign:

1. **Curve your fingers on both hands and place them together at the fingertips.**

2. **Open and close your hands several times and don't forget to make a menacing face all the while (see Figure 9-16).**

   Your hands are resembling an ALLIGATOR'S bite.

Figure 9-16: Snap! went the ALLIGATOR.

Chapter 10

Signing in the Great Outdoors

• •

• •

*M*ore than any other place in the whole wide world, my son Cole loves to go outside. It doesn't matter if the weather is hot, cold, rainy, or in between; he'll head out the door faster than a jackrabbit if we happen to leave it accessible. Maybe Cole likes the feeling of the hot sun or the cool wind, or maybe he just likes the fresh air or the extra room to run. Who knows? There's just something about going outside that floats his boat. (Pun intended.)

Many babies and toddlers feel the same way Cole does and share the same enthusiasm for going outside. And that's precisely the reason for this chapter. Here, I cover various signs you can use with your baby as you explore the great outdoors together.

C'mon, Baby, Take a Ride with Me

We all do it: transport ourselves continually from point A to point B. And as you know, there are numerous ways to get the job done. Sorting out what's what in modes of transportation can be hard for a baby. Signing can help your little sweetheart learn the difference between trains, planes, and, yes, automobiles.

Car

For a long time, my son Cole insisted on calling anything with wheels a BALL (see the nearby sidebar for details). We finally got through that mix-up, and now he insists that everything with wheels that moves is a CAR. Our van is a CAR, his sisters' bicycles are CARS, the garbage truck is a CAR, the red wagon in our backyard is a CAR, and even his stroller is a CAR.

It's a start.

Whether you're referring specifically to a car or to any other vehicle that has wheels and moves, sign the word CAR to aid your communication. "Do you want to take a ride in the CAR? Let's get in the CAR and go to the park! The CAR will take us there!" Here's the sign for CAR:

1. **Make two fists in front of you as if you're holding a steering wheel.**

2. **Move your hands up and down a few times as if you're turning a steering wheel (see Figure 10-1).**

Figure 10-1: Vroom, vroom. . . . Riding in the CAR.

By the way, I mention the word BALL in my story about Cole and his wheel confusion, and you may be wondering what the sign for BALL is. Mosey on over to the "Big Fun at the Community Park" section later in this chapter to find out.

Airplane

In my family, going to see some of the grandparents is an extremely long drive. Granted, without children the drive isn't so bad, but add my three kids to the mix and I'd rather be nearly anywhere else in the world than in the family van.

The wheels on the bus go 'round and 'round

While riding in the van one time, my son Cole signed and said BALL when there was no ball in sight. Following his glance, I realized he was referring to the wheels on a nearby vehicle. I affirmed that the wheels were the shape of a BALL, but I explained that the circles were actually wheels that go on a CAR. Cole continued to insist BALL — and continued to do so for a very long time. Oh well. To him BALL made sense, and eventually I did get him to put two and two — wheel and CAR — together.

Going off on a side road here, one reason I think kids like vehicles so much is that wheels going 'round and 'round are hypnotic, and the rumble of engines is calming. Doesn't matter to me what the cause is; who am I to argue with anything that keeps my kids still, and maybe even quiet, for a few minutes?

Now if my family *flies* to see the grandparents, we've got two things going for us:

✔ **The sheer novelty of an airplane ride:** The unique experience distracts my kids almost the entire flight and keeps them from screaming.

✔ **The extreme shortened "together time" in an enclosed space:** As long as someone doesn't poop in a diaper or training pants, we're good to go.

If you're planning to travel on one of those fabulous, shortened-together-time-in-an-enclosed-space, sanity-saving airplanes any time soon, start using the sign for AIRPLANE to get your baby in the know. And even if you're planning to keep your feet firmly on the ground, you can use the sign when your baby hears or sees a plane overhead.

Here's the sign for AIRPLANE:

1. **Make the I LOVE YOU sign by extending your thumb, index finger, and pinky of one hand (see Chapter 4).**

2. **Starting around your shoulder, move your I LOVE YOU hand up and over your head to the other shoulder (see Figure 10-2).**

Figure 10-2: Way up high AIRPLANE.

Bicycle

For her fourth birthday, my daughter Darby wanted nothing more than a pink bicycle with a backpack and water-bottle holder. Well, some of the grandparents indulged, and we now have a pink bicycle with a backpack and water-bottle holder in our garage. Darby's sister and brother think the bicycle is just as wonderful as Darby does, even though they're too small to ride it. Luckily, the sign for BICYCLE can also be used for a tricycle, a push toy, and a scooter, all of which are also in our garage and deemed wonderful by Darby's sister and brother.

Whether your go-go-go-getter rides a bike or a trike, or pushes a toy or a scooter, feel free to use the sign for BICYCLE to communicate what she's doing. Here's the sign for BICYCLE:

1. **Make two fists and place them close together in front of your body, palms down.**

2. **Rotate your fists as if they're pushing the pedals on a bicycle (see Figure 10-3).**

Figure 10-3: I like to ride my BICYCLE.

Train

Depending on where you live, TRAINS can be an important part of travel for your family. That's not the case in my neck of the woods, though, so my kids' experience with trains is limited to books, videos, and the local zoo. Additionally, my mom recently bought the kids wooden train whistles, so we also play train all over our house and actually whistle for passengers to board. Thanks, Mom. We're bringing the whistles to *your* house next time we visit so we can *all* have big fun.

When and if you're ready to play train with a real whistle at your house, I've actually seen train whistles in the toy section of the dollar store. Consider making it an outside game. And be sure to sign the word TRAIN all the while.

Likewise, if you use a TRAIN as a mode of transportation for your family, sign TRAIN when you're leaving the house, while you're waiting at the station, and when you're actually on the TRAIN. Same goes if you have a child with a TRAIN fascination — sign away while looking at train books or videos. Here's the sign:

1. **Form two ASL letter *Hs* by making two fists and extending the first two fingers of both hands (see Appendix A).**

2. **Place the fingertips of one *H* hand at the knuckle of the other *H* hand.**

3. **Move your fingertips back and forth on the fingers of the second hand (see Figure 10-4).**

   This movement mimics a TRAIN on railroad tracks.

Figure 10-4: Chugga chugga choo choo TRAIN!

Boat

One set of my kids' grandparents has a beach house on the coast in Galveston, Texas. The house is actually on one of the canals that eventually feeds into Galveston Bay. Needless to say, my kids love going to Pampu and GranJan's beach house, especially since last summer when they were first introduced to their grandparents' boat. What an experience for them! Between feeling the wind whip their hair and seeing the fish jump out of the water, my kids were absolutely *thrilled* with their first boat ride. And to think, prior to that day, they thought the sign for BOAT was limited to floating bathtub toys.

The magnificent train under the ground

A friend of mine, Beryt, and her son Josh, a proficient signing baby, were in a city with a subway, and Beryt realized that Josh was fascinated with the subway. Being the fabulous signing mom she is, Beryt took advantage of the situation. She showed Josh the sign for SUBWAY, right then and there. Because Beryt and her family don't live near a subway, and she knew they were headed for a city with a subway, she had looked the sign up ahead of time – just in case. Brilliant, isn't she? Feel free to follow her lead. She'll be thrilled to have inspired you.

So what do you do if you come across a situation and you don't know an appropriate sign? If you don't have the time or energy to look up signs before you go somewhere, use the signs you already know to your advantage. For example, instead of the sign for SUBWAY, you could show your fascinated baby that a subway is a TRAIN that goes UNDER the ground.

I cover the sign for TRAIN in the aptly named "Train" section of this chapter. Here's the cut-to-the-chase info for signing UNDER:

1. **Place one hand at chest level, in a closed-5 hand shape (see Chapter 3), palm down.**

2. **Make an ASL *A* (see Appendix A) with the other hand, and place it above (but not touching) your closed-5 hand.**

3. **Move the *A* hand from the top of the closed-5 hand to below the closed-5 hand.**

Look for ways to incorporate the sign for BOAT into your child's repertoire. Use the sign with any type of boat (row, paddle, speed, pontoon, ferry, and so on), whether it's real, on a video, or in the bathtub. (You may also want to have some companion signs in your back pocket. For example, the signs for SPLASH and BATH are in Chapter 7, and the sign for FISH is in Chapter 9.)

Here's the BOAT sign:

1. **Cup your hands together, pinky sides touching and thumb sides open.**

   Your cupped hands represent a BOAT.

2. **Move your hands up and down a bit (see Figure 10-5).**

   This movement represents a BOAT floating on water.

Figure 10-5: Row, row, row your BOAT. . . .

Moods of Mother Nature

Weather can have a profound effect on a child's (and a parent's) day. Rain or cold weather can put a damper on outside plans. Where I live, in southeast Texas, summertime heat forces my family indoors much more often than wintertime cold. Guess that's what we get for living here.

Next time Mother Nature throws your outside plans to the wind (pardon the pun) and you have to tell your little sweetie she can't go outside today, give her a reason with a sign. This section provides three basic signs to get you started: RAIN, SNOW, and WIND. Note, too, that you can use HOT and COLD to explain Mother Nature's mood. Those signs are covered in Chapter 6.

Rain

Rain, rain, go away, come again another day. This is a favorite song of my kids, especially when it's raining but even when it's not. Because my girls have raincoats, umbrellas, and rain boots, Darby and Aidan Elizabeth both think that every time it rains, they can go outside. Mentioning that the ground is too wet or that they might get wet is completely futile. "We won't get wet, Mommy. We'll wear our raincoats and rain boots, and we'll use our umbrellas while we splash in the puddles. We'll stay dry." Sure. Gotta love preschool logic.

When there's a rainstorm brewing outside your home, or when you catch a few drops while dashing to or from a store, show your baby how to sign RAIN. And while you're at it, sing a song about RAIN.

Here's the sign:

1. **Start with your hands open, palms down, fingers slightly curved, lifted above your head.**

2. **Bring your hands down, in short bounces, without wiggling your fingers (see Figure 10-6).**

Figure 10-6: RAIN, RAIN, go away. . . .

Snow

The last time it snowed in Houston, Texas, was Christmas Eve 2004. Before that, I think 1989 was the last time it snowed in Houston. I may be wrong on that date, but either way, snow is a rather big deal in my neck of the woods. That particular Christmas Eve was the first time my children had ever seen real snow, and my girls were absolutely thrilled. My son, however, was only 2 months old and couldn't have cared less.

Some of you are probably the complete opposite of my family. You see snow as much as or more than we see rain. If so, talk frequently about the snow with your child and use the sign to help him understand all that white stuff surrounding him. And while you're at it, sign that when it snows, that means it's COLD outside (see Chapter 6 for the sign for COLD). And if you live in a climate like mine, the sign is still great to use because even if the snow is just in picture books or on holiday cards, it holds big delight for children of all ages.

Here's the SNOW sign:

1. **Start with your hands open, palms down, fingers slightly curved, lifted above your head.**

   Note: This hand position is also the beginning step when making the RAIN sign (see the preceding section).

2. **Move your hands down, just as when signing RAIN, but wiggle your fingers instead of keeping them still (see Figure 10-7).**

Figure 10-7: Let it SNOW, let it SNOW, let it SNOW!

Wind

The area of the country my family lives in sometimes experiences massive destruction from wind due to hurricanes and tropical storms. Add those destructive types of wind to the normal gentle breezes that just cause the trees to sway, as well as the circulating breezes of continually running ceiling fans, and my kids have tons of opportunities to sign WIND.

You don't have to live in the hot, hot South or hurricane-prone areas or Tornado Alley to find opportunities to sign WIND. Great times to show your sweetie peetie the sign are when you're at the park feeling the wind on your face or when you're watching a tree or crops in a field move with the wind.

Any time she can actually feel or see what you're signing is a fantastic teachable moment because you're showing her a way to communicate whatever she happens to be interested in at the time. Here's the sign for WIND:

1. **Extend your hands, palms facing each other, in front of your body.**

2. **Move your hands and arms back and forth as if the WIND is blowing them (see Figure 10-8).**

Figure 10-8: She's like the WIND. . . .

Look! Up in the Sky!

One of the most important things children have taught me through the years, and especially my own children in recent years, is to look up. Children look up and down and all around while adults tend to simply look in the direction they're going (not bad to do, mind you, especially when you're driving). As an upshot of all their looking is that children tend to notice things adults miss, like a sleek airplane, a colorful bird, or a wealth of twinkling stars.

Take a moment, assuming you're not driving or walking right now, and look up. See what you may be missing. If you see a sleek plane, excitedly point at it and make the sign (covered earlier in this chapter). Same goes if you spot a colorful bird (see Chapter 9 for the signing details). Do you see the sun, moon, stars? Read on for the signs.

Sun

Looking up into the sun isn't a good thing to do. Usually, the only time I even notice the sun is when someone points out a sunset. My girls love to show me the sunset and their favorite colors in the sky. Darby and Aidan Elizabeth's favorite colors at the moment are purple and pink, respectively. (You can find color signs in Appendix C, if you're interested.)

Signing and singing together is a great way to introduce signs to your child and to reinforce signs you and your little one have learned or are learning. For example, you can sing a song about the sun and make the sign for SUN each time you sing the word. In addition to signing SUN while singing about it, you can sign SUN when showing your child a picture of the sun or sharing a sunset or sunrise together. Any of these modes are perfect for signing SUN.

Here's the sign:

1. **Make a flat-O hand shape (see Chapter 3) by first forming an O with your fingers and thumb and then flattening them out so that it looks like a deflated balloon, and have your fingertips pointing down.**

2. **Using your fingertips as a writing utensil, draw a circle in the air.**

   You're drawing the sun here.

3. Open your fingers so that your palm is facing the floor (see Figure 10-9).

The open fingers facing down represent the sun's rays shining down.

Figure 10-9: Mr. SUN, please shine down on me!

Moon

Much safer to look at than the sun, the moon is a great source of fascination for my kids. While riding in the van recently, my 4-year-old, Darby, shouted at the top of her lungs, "Look, Mom! The moon is a *C* tonight!"

At that point, her younger sister, Aidan Elizabeth, showed baby brother Cole the sign for MOON. "Look, Cole, this is the sign for MOON." Gotta love those signing siblings.

Some fantastic books about the moon are available for young children, and some are even in board-book format to lengthen their durability. I have one board book about the moon that's on its third child. Talk about a lasting investment!

Anyway, when you're looking at a book that shows a picture of the moon, or when you're riding in the car and see the moon (*and* someone else is driving), or when your baby looks at the moon and signs BALL (which I cover later in this chapter), show her the sign for MOON:

1. **Make a *C* hand shape with one hand (see Appendix A).**

2. **Place the *C* hand shape at your eye.**

3. **Keeping the *C* hand shape, move your hand up above your head (see Figure 10-10).**

   This movement represents looking up at the moon.

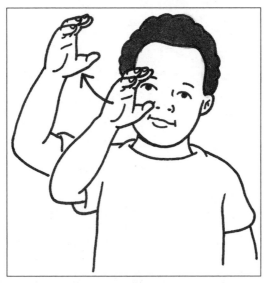

Figure 10-10: Hey diddle diddle . . . the cow jumped over the MOON.

Stars

Singing about twinkling stars is one of my daughter Aidan Elizabeth's favorite pastimes. It may stem from the fact that big sis Darby used to sing the song to her when Aidan Elizabeth was a baby. Consequently, every time Aidan Elizabeth sees a crying baby, she goes over to the baby and sings "Twinkle, Twinkle Little Star." Sometimes it works, sometimes it doesn't, but I absolutely applaud the effort.

When you sing about twinkling stars to your shining star, or if you happen to live in a place where you can actually see stars in the night sky, show her the STAR sign. Here it is:

1. **Extend your index fingers on both hands and place them side by side, fingertips pointing up.**

2. **Alternating fingers, move one finger higher than the other several times (see Figure 10-11).**

   Imagine you're counting the STARS in the sky, one by one.

Figure 10-11: Twinkle, twinkle, little STAR.

Big Fun at the Community Park

Several community parks are near my house, and my family enjoys visiting and picnicking at them on a regular basis. We always have a blast on the swings and slides, and my kids love the chance to see friends there and to cool off under a big shade tree. As a side note, we have some of the same playground equipment (and more) in our backyard, and my girls have begun affectionately calling our backyard Watson World. Must've heard that one from their daddy.

Maybe you and yours have a nearby park or a roomy backyard to enjoy. When you're catching your bundle of energy at the end of the slide or pushing her in the swing, show her the signs for whatever you're doing and then ask her if she wants MORE (the sign for MORE is in Chapter 5).

Play

You can use the sign for PLAY in a wide variety of settings, such as at the park or at the house or anywhere else baby is feeling playful. To introduce the sign for PLAY, say something like "I wonder what you want to PLAY with today. Do you want to PLAY with your BALL or your CAR today?" or "Let's PLAY together. How about we PLAY peek-a-boo? Where's BABY?" (I cover the signs for BALL and CAR in this chapter, and I cover the sign for BABY in Chapter 4.)

However you decide to use it, the sign for PLAY is a great way to communicate fun to your baby. Here's how to make the sign:

1. **Make the ASL letter *Y* with both hands, palms facing your body (see appendix A).**

   To form the letter Y, make a fist and then extend your thumb and pinkie finger.

2. **Shake both hands a few times in a PLAYful manner (see Figure 10-12).**

Figure 10-12: Wanna PLAY?

Ball

So you're planning an afternoon at the park and trying to decide whether you should pack anything more than a diaper bag, a big blanket to drape across the grass, and a bag of snacks and sippy drinks. Well, consider that parks usually have wide open spaces . . . and lots of children. Sounds like a great opportunity to play with a big, bouncy ball.

Whether you're taking your big, bouncy ball to the park or your own backyard, let junior know he's in for big fun by saying and signing what's going on. Here's the sign for BALL:

1. **Using loose open hands, face your palms toward each other, roughly shoulder-width apart.**

2. **Pull your hands out and bounce them back in a few times as if you're holding a ball (see Figure 10-13).**

Figure 10-13: Bouncy, bouncy BALL!

Swing

Ahh, the power of a swing. When Aidan Elizabeth was a baby, I'm not sure my husband and I would've survived without a baby swing. Sometimes the swing was the only thing that calmed her fussy little self down. Even now, all three of my kids would be content to spend the entire day being pushed on the backyard or playground swing.

If you happen to have a fussy baby or toddler at your house, try the swing. If she's old enough to understand, try to distract her from crying by suggesting and signing that she and you go outside to play on the swing. Now, please don't mention going outside to play on the swing if you don't have time to actually follow through. That's opening up a whole new can of worms. But if you've got the time, this tactic is definitely worth a shot.

And, of course, say and sign SWING on non-fussy occasions, too. When spending quality time with your sweetie at the park or in your own backyard, feel free to sign away. Here's how:

1. **Make a *C* with one hand (see Appendix A).**

2. **Hook the first two fingers of your other hand over the thumb of your *C* hand.**

3. **Now move your hands forward and back as if they were a swing (see Figure 10-14).**

Figure 10-14: SWING me higher, Daddy!

Slide

One of the things my girls love to do is make "trains" as they're sliding down a slide. An extra-fun element is added when little brother joins them. Whipping through the air down a slide is usually big fun no matter what, but adding extra people for a "train" takes big fun through the roof.

At the park or in your own backyard, say and sign SLIDE whenever your little darling is getting ready to take the plunge. Here's the sign for SLIDE:

1. **Extend one hand, palm up.**

2. **With the other hand, make an ASL *V* by extending your first two fingers (see Appendix A).**

3. **Now bend those fingers, and turn your palm face up.**

4. **Place the back of your bent-*V* hand at the heel of your other hand's open palm and move the bent-*V* hand forward quickly, sliding it on your open palm (see Figure 10-15).**

Figure 10-15: SLIDE . . . whee!

The Wonders of Your Own Backyard

Any time they're outside, kids tend to notice more things than adults do. I can't tell you how many times one of my kids has made an excited yelp and shown me ants in the dirt or a bird in the tree that I had been totally oblivious to.

When you take your little one to your backyard or on a walk through your neighborhood, tune in to the wonders he points out to you. And go ahead and show him the sign for whatever he's interested in. This section covers signs for three items that are common to most backyards: trees, flowers, and good old-fashioned, fun-to-play-in dirt.

Trees

You can climb in them, they provide cool shade on hot sunny days, and they add beauty to their surroundings. And trees are an easy focal point for children due to the sheer height difference between the two. Anything towering over a young'un is sure to catch her attention.

Next time you see your child staring at tree branches or seeking shelter from the blazing sun under a shady tree, show her the sign for TREE:

1. **Place the elbow of one arm on the hand of the other.**

   Your elbow represents the base of a tree; your arm, the trunk; and your fingers, the branches.

2. **Using the arm that's representing a tree, twist your hand at the wrist a few times (see Figure 10-16).**

   This action represents the movement of tree branches.

Flower

As a parent, one of the sweetest joys in my life is when my girls bring me flowers that they find growing outside. They always say, "I love you," when they hand me a flower. In those sweet moments, it's difficult for me to remember why they sometimes drive me crazy. Of course, I'm quickly reminded just how crazy they can drive me when I realize the flowers they just brought me are from a flower bed I've been slaving over.

Figure 10-16: TREE, wonderful TREE!

The next time your child notices a flower in your backyard or brings you one from the very flower bed you've been slaving over all summer long, smile and show him the sign for FLOWER. "Oooh, what a pretty FLOWER! Let's smell the pretty FLOWER and put the FLOWER in a vase with WATER!" You can find the sign for WATER in Chapter 7, and you can find the sign for FLOWER right here:

1. **Using a flat-O hand shape (see Chapter 3), place your fingertips to the right of your nose.**

2. **Move your hand in an arc around to the left so that your fingertips are touching the left side of your nose (see Figure 10-17).**

   Imagine you're smelling a flower, first with your right nostril and then with your left.

Figure 10-17: Mmmm, a sweet-smelling FLOWER.

Dirt

Eventually, you'll experience it with your baby or toddler. Every parent I know has at least one child who has tasted dirt. Yummy.

Both of my girls have tried dirt as a matter of experimentation. However, my son has been caught several times *shoving* dirt in his mouth. He always grins widely, showing the dirt among his teeth, and signs DIRT for his parents. He just wants us to be proud. Oh, well, I guess there are worse things. . . .

You can find DIRT just about everywhere you go, including your own backyard. And it can be the bane of your existence if you have hard floors in your house and active, outdoorsy children. Out and in, out and in, tracking up the floors again.

If you can't beat 'em, join 'em. In other words, if you find your little one fascinated by DIRT, show her the sign and show her how to make dust in the wind. Or a mud pie. With any luck, she won't eat it. Here's the sign for DIRT:

1. **Make the flat-O hand shape with both hands (see Chapter 3), palms up.**

2. **Rub your fingertips with your thumbs (see Figure 10-18).**

   Imagine you have dusty dirt falling through your hands.

Figure 10-18: DIRT. Is it food or not, Mommy?

Part IV
Now We're Talking

The 5th Wave
By Rich Tennant

"We sign with the baby all the time. This morning I was reading her my latest manuscript and she signed the words for, 'fresh', 'insightful' and 'poignant'."

In this part . . .

*W*hen you and your baby have a solid set of signs under your belt, you may begin to wonder, "Where do we go from here?" Or perhaps, after baby begins to talk, you may wonder, "Do I go anywhere from here? Or is it time to quit signing?"

The decisions you make are a matter of personal choice. However, as the mother of three signing children, and as a former teacher, I have strong feelings on this subject. On the basis of these feelings, I have a heartfelt request: *Please* keep signing with your little one, even when she's no longer a baby. I explain why in this part: The benefits of continued signing are worth the effort. In addition, I introduce sign combinations, the baby-signing equivalent to sentences. I also answer some common questions about struggles and stumbling blocks you may encounter along the baby-signing journey.

Chapter 11

Signing Sentences

· ·

· ·

*W*hen I was pregnant with my first child, I was looking at a friend's scrapbook of her 2½-year-old, Megan, and I laughed out loud when I got to the page commemorating Megan's first sentence, "I sum gapes." (Those without small children know this sentence as "I want some grapes.") Megan made this statement while she was standing outside the refrigerator and attempting to open it. Beyond thinking it was cute, I thought, "Holy cow! This milestone hadn't even occurred to me."

To this day, I still haven't scrapbooked any of my three children's milestones (although I've had lofty intentions), but I do recall all three of my children's first sign sentences. Whether you're a scrapbooking parent or not, among the treasured memories you'll cherish of your signing baby will be his first signed sentence.

What's a Sign Sentence?

More than one sign within a few seconds is essentially a signed sentence — but in this sense, the term *sentence* is used loosely. Just as "I sum gapes" constitutes a sentence for a toddler, so do the signed words EAT MORE or PLAY BALL.

Just as you wouldn't expect a toddler's sentence to be grammatically correct (like "May I please have some grapes?"), don't expect your baby to sign, "I would like to eat more food, please." In other words, don't expect your baby to sign every word of the sentence he's trying to communicate. (That's not how American Sign Language works anyway.) Instead, watch for and model for baby the use of any two or more signs together to express a single desire or thought.

Signing sentences will occur naturally in conversations with your baby, but that's not to say you should start out with sign sentences. Over time your signing conversations with your baby will evolve to this point. When you and baby have developed a large enough sign vocabulary to consider combining signs to make a sentence, it's probably time to start trying.

Is Signing Sentences Really a Big Deal?

You may be wondering, "What's so important about sign sentences?" Your baby can sign EAT, and she can sign MORE. Why should you be excited if she signs EAT MORE?

Consider verbal communication: My friend instinctively recognized her daughter's ability to say "I sum gapes" as a developmental leap from what she had done previously, which was to stand in front of the refrigerator, pointing, grunting, and screaming "Gape!" The ability to string words together in a meaningful way is a step forward in communication, be it verbal or signed. For a baby, the ability to express her thoughts with more than one word or sign indicates that her brain is developing — and so are her abilities to think, understand, and communicate.

Communication is an evolving skill. None of us is born quoting Shakespeare. (In fact, some of us never quite get there, thank you very much.) We begin with monosyllabic tones (think Tim Allen's caveman impression on *Home Improvement*), step up to intelligible singular words, move ahead to broken sentences, and then eventually (if our eighth-grade grammar teacher is at all successful) learn proper sentence structure. As the parent of a signing baby, you can celebrate baby's first sign sentence (which will probably come along long before her first sentence) for exactly what it is: a true milestone in her growth and development, whether you scrapbook it or not.

So When and How Do I Begin?

Know up front that sign sentences are not a starting point. This is one of the few chapters in this book that expects you and baby to have some previous signing under your belts. If you're just starting to sign with your baby and you've turned to this chapter as a jumping-in point, come back later. For now, refer to the book's Introduction for suggestions on where to begin. If you've already tried your hand at some other chapters and you and your baby are signing a bit, stay right here — and congratulations on the progress you and baby have made so far!

Now that baby has a few signs in his vocabulary, begin to consider which of these signs might go together to form sentences. If baby doesn't know it yet, this would be a great time to introduce the sign for MORE (see Chapter 5 or the following section), because MORE can be used with many other signs to form meaningful sign sentences. After you've identified the possible sign combinations within baby's sign vocabulary, begin to use these sentences with baby in the appropriate contexts. For example, if baby is restless at the dinner table, use your signs to ask if he wants to EAT MORE, or if he is FINISHED and wants to PLAY. (Check out the following section for various sign-sentence examples so you can get a good feel for when and how to do it.)

Now remember, you're entering a new stage in baby's signed communication. Just as you didn't expect him to sign back to you that first day, don't expect him to begin signing sentences right away. The general rules for signing with baby apply to combining signs with baby: focus on *only a few* sentences, look for the right time to use them, and be consistent. Take heart: At this point your baby is probably already thinking in sentences, so it won't be long before he's signing them.

Looking at a Few Sign Sentences

Obviously, signs — just like words — can be combined in a limitless number of ways. However, among signing babies, I've observed a few common sign-sentence families. I cover some of them in this section and hope you find them helpful.

The sign-sentence families presented in this chapter are generalizations, and they're far from being all-inclusive. In fact, many sign sentences defy all attempts at classification. I'm sure you and your baby will come up with many original sign sentences together.

MORE sentences

The sign MORE can go with many, many, *many* different things. Case in point: The first sign sentence from Aidan Elizabeth, my second child, was MORE ELEPHANT. Although my home often resembles a zoo, I've never seen any elephants running around, so this one took a while to figure out. In the end, Aidan Elizabeth wanted to watch more of a zoo video that features elephants.

Likewise, your baby's first sign sentence may well be MORE combined with something she really loves.

For a practical example from this family of sign sentences, consider the sign sentence MORE BUBBLES. If your little one signs this sentence, she might mean your bubble machine needs refilling or you just need to blow faster.

To make this sign sentence, follow these steps:

1. **Using both hands, make two flat-O hand shapes (see Chapter 3).**

2. **Repeatedly touch the fingertips of both hands (see the top illustration in Figure 11-1).**

   You've just signed MORE.

3. **Using the flat-O hand shapes from the sign for MORE, point the fingertips of both hands up.**

4. **Open and close your hands while alternately moving them up and down in front of your body (see the bottom illustration in Figure 11-1).**

   You've just signed BUBBLES to go along with MORE. Easy peasy.

EAT sentences

Eating is a big part of baby's life. Heck, it's a big part of *mine*. Like me, my babies love to eat, but there are some things they enjoy eating more than others. So in other words, just because your baby wants to eat, don't expect him to turn flips when you put that bowl of puréed peas in front of him. With the EAT family of sign sentences, your baby can be more specific, communicating not only *that* he wants to eat but *what* he wants to eat.

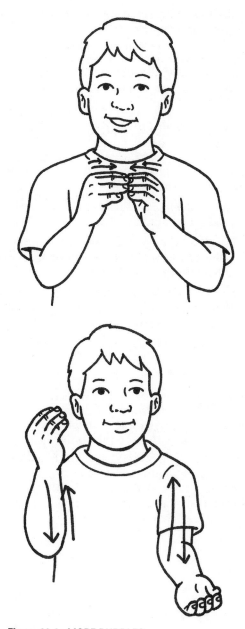

Figure 11-1: MORE BUBBLES.

If your baby loves cookies as much as my three, he'll appreciate knowing the sign sentence EAT COOKIE, even if, like me, you rarely indulge his wishes. To make the sign combo for EAT COOKIE, follow these steps:

1. **Make a flat-O hand shape with one hand (see Chapter 3).**

2. **Touch the fingertips of your flat-O hand shape to your mouth repeatedly (see the top drawing in Figure 11-2).**

   You've just signed EAT.

3. **Hold out one hand, palm open and facing up, mimicking rolled-out cookie dough.**

4. **Form a *C* hand shape (see Appendix A) with your other hand, mimicking a cookie cutter.**

5. **Lower your *C* hand, fingers and thumb pointing down, onto the palm of your opposite hand and then raise, twist, and lower your *C* hand again, as if you're using a cookie cutter to cut out cookie shapes (see the bottom drawing in Figure 11-2).**

   You've just signed COOKIE to go along with EAT.

PLAY sentences

Baby loves to play. In fact, for now that's her job. Through her imaginative play, baby is learning and practicing how to relate to the world around her. And just as with eating, there are some things baby enjoys playing with more than others. Using the PLAY family of sign sentences, baby can let you know the object of her playtime desires.

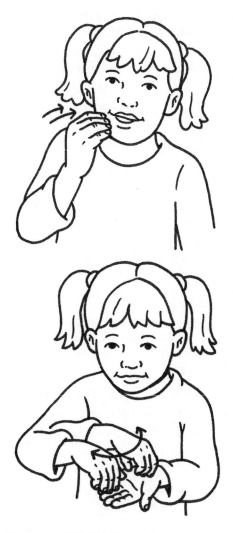

Figure 11-2: EAT COOKIE.

"Play ball!" is how an umpire signals the beginning of a baseball game. For your baby, however, the sign sentence PLAY BALL is how she lets you know she wants to play with her favorite toy. That is, if she loves balls as much as my youngest, Cole. Here's how to sign PLAY BALL:

1. **Make the ASL letter *Y* (see Appendix A) with both hands, palms facing your body.**

2. **Shake both hands a few times in a playful manner (see the top drawing in Figure 11-3).**

    You've just signed PLAY.

3. **Using loose open hands, face your palms toward each other, roughly shoulder-width apart.**

4. **Pull your hands out and bounce them back in a few times as if you're holding a ball (see the bottom drawing in Figure 11-3).**

   You've just signed BALL to go along with PLAY.

PLEASE sentences

The magic word. You were probably taught from an early age that in order to get something you wanted, you had to say *please*. And you're probably passing this mannerly gesture on to your little one. It's so ingrained in my kids that any time they make a request, they automatically follow up with "please" in both sign and speaking. I guess we do whatever it takes to make sure they're polite. Only time will tell.

My youngest, Cole, likes to combine the sign for PLEASE with the sign for DRINK, as this is a frequent request of his. In fact, here's an example of a *three*-sign sentence that Cole often uses: MORE DRINK PLEASE. Yes, I'm aware that this sentence can go in the MORE family, too. Regardless of how you categorize it, here's how to make the sign sentence:

1. **Using both hands, make two flat-O hand shapes (see Chapter 3).**

2. **Repeatedly touch the fingertips of both hands (see the top drawing in Figure 11-4).**

   You've just signed MORE.

3. **Form an ASL *C* (see Appendix A) with one hand and hold it as if you're holding a drink.**

4. **Mimic drinking by bringing your hand to your mouth and tilting it several times (see the middle drawing in Figure 11-4).**

   You've just signed DRINK to go along with MORE.

5. **Place your palm flat against your chest as though you're about to say the Pledge of Allegiance.**

6. **Make a circle with your palm on your chest with a quizzical look on your face (see the bottom drawing in Figure 11-4).**

   You've just signed PLEASE to go along with MORE DRINK.

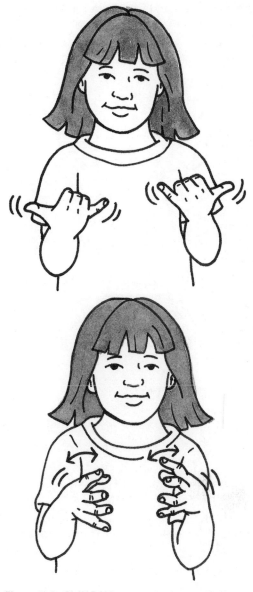

Figure 11-3: PLAY BALL.

Figure 11-4: MORE DRINK PLEASE.

Chapter 12

Overcoming Stumbling Blocks

In This Chapter

▶ Figuring out what to do when there's a problem

▶ Getting back on track and keeping the signing going with baby

*W*ell, it was bound to happen. A problem or two has popped up, and you're ready to throw in the towel on this signing-with-baby business. Well, hold off until you read this chapter. It provides answers to some of the questions I hear frequently. This info will help get you back on track, with your towel tucked back in the linen closet.

Why Isn't Baby Signing Back?

Little pumpkin is busy right now. She's learning to sit up, crawl, and walk — or some combination thereof. She has a lot on her mind, and her attention may be focused elsewhere. If your baby isn't signing back, consider the following sections.

Maybe you're overwhelming baby with too many signs

Processing lots of signs at once is more than baby's brain can handle. You should never be working on more than a handful of new signs at any given time. What's a new sign? Any sign that she hasn't signed back yet. So if you're just beginning, work on only a few initial signs (see Chapter 3 for more information on choosing these signs).

If you've been at it a little while, and baby has signed a few signs back to you, work on those signs *plus* a handful of new ones. This method is how, over time, baby builds her sign vocabulary — not by being bombarded with a sign for everything in her world. (For related info, see the section "When Do I Add More Signs?" later in this chapter.)

Maybe the signs you're using aren't for the things that excite and interest baby

The signs you're introducing to your baby must also be ones he's interested in. He may not be crazy about stars right now, for example. In fact, depending on his age, his vision may not even be developed enough to differentiate stars from the rest of the night sky. So why should he sign STAR?

As babies, all three of my kids were fascinated by the light when they looked up toward the ceiling. Blew me away. I mean, who cares about the lights unless there's a bulb out? But I found that the sign for LIGHT (see Chapter 7) was a good fit for their interests.

Toddlers often have a favorite toy. For my 18-month-old son, Cole, his favorite — at the moment — is his toy train, so the sign for TRAIN (see Chapter 10) is in the repertoire for him. Pay attention to your little one, and he'll reveal his current passions to you.

Maybe baby is trying to sign, but you just don't realize it

Know upfront that your baby's initial attempts won't mirror your signs or even the pictures in this book. Consider, for example, the sign for HELP (see Chapter 6). It resembles a thumbs-up gesture with one hand as it rests in the palm of your other hand. But on my son Cole's hands, it's an elbow that rests in the palm of one hand while the other hand waves. *That* gesture happens to look an awful lot like the sign for TREE (see Chapter 10), so how do I know Cole is signing HELP and not TREE? Context is crucial, as well as the frequency with which Cole repeats his rendition of HELP.

So, if you're working on the sign for, say, BALL with baby (see Chapter 10), pay extra attention whenever she's in the vicinity of a ball. Does she make consistent movements with her hands that even remotely (and it may be *very* remotely) resemble the sign you're showing her? If so, then she's signing! And she's probably wondering why you don't understand her. After all, in her mind, her sign is identical to yours.

What If I'm the Only One Who Signs with Baby?

For whatever reason, baby's other parent, grandparents, and/or other caregivers may choose not to sign with him, and sometimes there's nothing you can do to convince them otherwise.

Have you shown them the ten reasons to sign with your baby in Chapter 14? If you have and they still refuse to sign with baby, know that it's their loss. Your little one will figure out how to sign even if you're the only one who signs with him. Plus, imagine how your bond with baby will be strengthened by your efforts and commitment to signing.

And don't lose hope for the other people in baby's life who refuse to sign. I've seen more than one naysayer turn on a dime when they see a baby communicate a want or need through sign language. For example, the staff at my church's nursery used to roll their eyes at the idea of signing with babies. Now, thanks to my three little signers, the nursery staff is constantly asking me and my husband (and sometimes our 3-year-old and 4-year-old) to interpret signs our little ones use, to show them new signs to work on with other kids, and for general information about signing with babies. So the first time your little one signs, he just might change a few minds.

Why Does Baby Use the Same Sign for Everything?

My poor husband was frustrated for weeks as our youngest, Cole, our only son, went through a phase of calling his dad *mommy*. We had heard him earlier refer to his father as *da, da-da,* and *daddy,* so we knew he understood the difference and could say it as well as sign it. In fact, he would sign DADDY (see Chapter 4) as he called my husband *mommy*. You can imagine my husband's reaction — as well as my own giggling, delighted one. In fact, the reaction he received probably had a great deal to do with why Cole continued to call his father *mommy*.

If your little one is applying the same sign to several objects, the reasoning is probably similar. She was so delighted by the positive reaction she received when she used the sign appropriately that she decided to try the sign with something else. Who can blame her? She probably didn't get the same response, but the response she got, she liked. In search of more reaction, she continues to apply that same sign to other objects.

What can you do? First, continue to use the correct signs for objects you're currently working on. Second, fight the urge to react when baby misapplies a sign she knows. Though you may not realize it, your attempts to correct her may be just the reaction baby is seeking, and may even be the reason she knowingly used the incorrect sign in the first place. If baby doesn't get the response she's seeking, chances are she'll return to using the sign appropriately.

And speaking of which, Cole stopped calling his dad *mommy* at about the same time my husband resigned himself to the fact that his only son would call him *mommy* for the rest of their lives.

Why Doesn't Baby Sign Anymore?

Your signing baby no longer signs, and you want to know what that means. Well, it doesn't mean that he doesn't understand signing. It simply means he's busy. He's busy learning to push the wagon or climb on the sofa. Or he's busy noticing the wind or the sound of the kitchen clock. For now, communicating with his outside world has taken a back seat to more pressing matters.

What can you do? First of all, keep signing. Baby will assimilate the new experiences and information that currently hold his attention. After he does, he'll want to pick up signing again because you've continued to sign with him. To make the most of this hiatus, focus on the things that are keeping him busy right now. If he stops in his tracks to feel the wind blow against his cheek, then show him the sign for WIND (see Chapter 10). When he's ready to sign again, make WIND one of the handful of new signs you work on with him.

How do you know when baby's ready to sign again? If you continue to sign to him throughout his break from signing, he'll surprise you one day and simply begin to sign back again, as though he never skipped a beat. If you stop signing because baby seems to have taken a break, then your baby may never pick up signing again.

When Do 1 Add More Signs?

Repeat after me: "I will *not* ask my baby to process too many new signs at once." This point is crucial. Otherwise, she'll become overwhelmed by the task and may shut down and ignore signing altogether.

You — and the other signers in her life — should only show your baby the signs she knows and the new signs she's working on. Anything more than a handful of the latter is too much.

How does baby's sign vocabulary grow? As she begins to repeat a sign back to you, think about another new sign to work on. Or perhaps she's beginning to show a great deal of interest in a certain object. Don't miss this opportunity. Go ahead and replace a current new sign that you're working on — one that baby doesn't seem as interested in — with the sign for this new interest. You can just revisit the sign you've replaced later, when baby's ready. That said, be careful not to shuffle signs in and out of your list of signs to work on *too* frequently. Trying to stick with a new sign until baby knows it is important.

Instead of doing the shuffle, you may simply decide to add the sign for a new item of interest to your current handful of new signs to work on. That's fine. There is no magic number of signs to include in your handful. Again, just exercise caution when adding new signs. Baby is interested in a lot of different things from day to day. As a result, your handful of signs can easily become an armful before you realize it.

The bottom line? Take your cues from your baby.

What If My Baby Isn't Talking, but He's Signing like Crazy?

First off, take a deep breath. Rejoice in the fact that your baby is communicating with you in some fashion! Talk to your doctor about speech development norms and voice your concerns. Do some family research. Were you or baby's other parent a late talker? Sometimes these tendencies run in families. Regardless, if your parental instinct is telling you that something's wrong, listen to it. Plenty of places are available to get answers in the form of information or even testing.

No matter what, under no circumstances allow anyone to tell you that the reason he's not talking is due to the signing. Yes, studies have shown that signing has an impact on a baby's speech development — but this impact is a *positive* one. Signing won't slow your baby's speech development; it will *enhance* your baby's speech development. Chances are, he would've had the speech-delay issues whether you signed with him or not. And imagine how much more difficult things would be if you weren't signing with him. (I also briefly cover this issue in Chapter 1. And you may want to check out the sidebar in that chapter about my own daughter's speech delay.)

Chapter 13

How Long Do We Keep This Up?

*E*ventually, you'll get to a point where you'll stop signing very much with your little one. It may be because he's started speaking more and signing isn't as necessary for communication, or it may be because you've just had too much going on to be consistent with signing with him. At this point, you'll probably begin to wonder how much longer you should sign with your baby, toddler, or even preschooler.

The reality here is that you don't need to keep signing if your only goal has been to interact more specifically with your nonverbal baby or toddler. But many families discover that they're having such a good time interacting with each other through signs that they're not ready to quit.

Trust me, there's nothing more incredible than a 4-year-old who actively knows and uses over 300 signs on a daily basis. My 4-year-old came to me just this morning and whispered in my ear that she'd only be using signs today. No words from her mouth. We'll see how long it lasts. Even if she doesn't make it for 15 minutes, her family has given her the option to do it if she so desires.

In addition to the fun your child will have by continuing the signing journey, he'll receive some long-term benefits as well. This chapter explains what they are.

Better Student All Around

An obvious long-term benefit of signing is that kids who sign have an additional way to communicate. According to Dr. Marilyn Daniels, author of *Dancing with Words,* as signing kids get older, sometimes they don't have a word in their spoken vocabulary but *do* have that word in their sign vocabulary, enabling them to get their point across and feel satisfied with their communication.

That's fine and good in itself, but consider what else Dr. Daniels found: She did extensive research following signing babies through sixth grade, and what she found was that sixth graders who had signed as infants and toddlers and continued using sign language were *better students all around,* scoring higher on tests and having better performance levels in the classroom.

According to Dr. Daniels's Web site (www.marilyndaniels.com), her research shows "how sign language can be used to improve hearing children's English vocabulary, reading ability, spelling proficiency, self-esteem, and comfort with expressing emotions."

Improved language arts skills

American Sign Language (ASL) has roughly one sign to every eight or nine English words. So how on Earth can Dr. Daniels claim that sign language affects vocabulary, reading, and spelling? Well, for one thing, a signer often has to figure out a different sign to use for a word that doesn't have an actual sign. Most times the signer ends up having to use a synonym of the original word, so the signer ends up with a bigger vocabulary as a result.

For example, a month before my daughter Aidan Elizabeth turned 2 years old, and several months *before* she was diagnosed with a speech delay, my family was driving down a freeway. We passed a car dealership with a large pink gorilla on its roof. Newly 3-year-old daughter Darby said, "Look, Mommy, that gorilla is giant!" I said, "You're right, that is a big gorilla." Aidan Elizabeth said, "It huge!" and signed the synonym BIG. Her father and I were completely blown away.

Consider also that many ASL signs begin with an individual letter sign. This framework aids in spelling proficiency as children learn the ASL alphabet and then as they learn to spell words. If children sign and spell out loud their spelling words, they have a greater chance of remembering and actually learning those words.

You're asking *me?*

My children love that adults — who are usually the ones in an authoritative position — ask *them* how to do certain signs. It really boosts the kids' self-esteem. Granted, at first the adults usually ask me if the signs are correct, but they quickly stop asking because they realize my kids really do know their stuff. Well, sometimes the adults still have to seek a *little* clarification when my 18-month-old signs, itty-bitty hands and all.

With these examples, you can begin to connect the dots between signing and long-term benefits to language arts skills.

Improved self-esteem and comfort expressing emotions

As for how sign language can improve self-esteem and comfort with expressing emotions, consider my take: When an adult works with a child through signing, the adult is paying lots of extra attention to the child by watching the child's movements and reading his emotions. The child feels validated because an adult is taking the time to understand him.

And identifying feelings for children as they are expressed will help them in the long run be better communicators and more comfortable expressing their emotions. Signing the feelings will enhance communication even more.

Higher IQ and Less ADD/ADHD

Hand in hand with helping children be better students all around, continuing the signing journey also helps children's IQ scores and their ability to combat Attention Deficit Disorder/Attention Deficit Hyperactivity Disorder (ADD/ADHD).

Higher IQ scores

Although boosting your sweetie's brain power shouldn't be the only reason you sign with her, it is absolutely an added bonus.

Dr. Linda Acredolo and Dr. Sarah Goodwyn, authors of *Baby Signs,* did some research back in the early 1980s that provided some astounding results. Children who signed as babies scored an average of 12 points higher on IQ tests than their non-signing peers. So beyond the immediate benefits of communicating with your baby, in less than ten years, you and your baby will be reaping even more benefits.

Less ADD/ADHD

This is a strong claim — and it doesn't promise your kid won't have ADD/ADHD. It is, however, a way to potentially reduce a child's ADD/ADHD. Signing children as a whole seem to have a better handle on expressing their feelings because they have an additional outlet to do so. Additionally, ADD/ADHD children often have a difficult time being still or focusing on one thing. Because signing is a kinesthetic activity, it gives children's hands something to do, instead of acting out. Signing helps children focus better because it allows them to physically process information with their hands and bodies. Dr. Daniels followed signing babies through sixth grade and saw a large variant in ADD/ADHD between signing children and non-signing children.

Stronger Sibling Relationships

Not much research has been done on this subject, at least that I can find, so I'm going to use my experience with my own children here. Research abounds on how signing can strengthen the relationship between parents and children. Well, signing can also strengthen the relationship between siblings.

Big sis Darby taught little sis Aidan Elizabeth colors with sign. I have a video of them at around 3 and 2 years of age where Aidan Elizabeth was signing WHAT COLOR and holding up a crayon and Darby was signing back RED as she spoke the word.

I also have a video of Darby and Aidan Elizabeth showing signs to little bro Cole, who was only weeks old at the time — they were trying to make him do the signs as well. "Cole, you're a BOY. Darby is a GIRL. Aidan Elizabeth is a GIRL." "Cole, this is how you sign COOKIE." "Cole, this is how you sign POTTY." (We must have our priorities after all.)

All the time at my house, the kids go up to each other, tap the other on the shoulder, and sign whatever they want to communicate. "TIME to GO to DANCE!"

I'm looking out for you, sister

Sixteen-month-old signing baby Avery was in her high chair. Mom was feeding her the usual foods, and Avery was fussing and refusing them all.

Mom said and signed, "Do you want some GRAPES?" No.

"Do you want some MILK?" No.

"Do you want a CRACKER?" No.

"Do you want a BANANA?" No.

Things were getting frustrating fast and going nowhere.

Three-year-old big brother, Carter, stepped in as he signed and asked, "Avery, do you want some CAKE?"

Mom looked at Carter and laughed. Avery laughed. Carter laughed. Fussy situation diverted.

Carter used signs to help his mom take care of his little sister. He was modeling mom's behavior as many 3-year-olds do in giving care to babies. This just happened to be a signing family for Carter to model. I bet they all remembered the sign for CAKE from there on out. And I believe that by good-naturedly signing with his sister, Carter is also strengthening his relationship with her.

And although they're usually perfect angels, on occasion, they have to sit in timeout. I've begun catching them, especially if more than one is in timeout at the same time, signing back and forth to each other. So now the new rule is "You may not talk *or* sign while you're in timeout."

I guess the bottom line I'm trying to express is

They sign, therefore they bond.

Signing is a special form of communication that brothers and sisters can share together, which in the process strengthens their relationship.

Part V
The Part of Tens

The 5th Wave   By Rich Tennant

"Your baby's fussiness, whining and general discontent aren't anything to worry about. They should clear up on their own in about 18 years."

In this part . . .

With just about anything in life, if you pose the same question to ten different people, you'll get ten different answers. Keep that thought in mind when perusing this part of the book. Each list is my attempt to offer the ten best choices related to some important topics about baby signing. Here, you find ten reasons to sign with your baby, ten signs you and your baby should know, ten songs you can sign with baby, and ten resources to help you along the baby-signing path. Personally, I believe Part V alone is worth the price you paid for the whole book!

Chapter 14

Ten Reasons to Sign with Baby

▶ Knowing what to tell the doubters when they ask why you sign

▶ Finding reasons to give baby's grandparents to convince them to sign

▶ Getting some convincing reasons to do this whole signing-with-baby thing

*M*aybe you (or your spouse or significant other) picked this book up, brought it home, and then let it just sit there gathering dust — you've been awfully busy with that baby, after all — and now you're wondering why you (or said spouse or significant other) brought it home in the first place.

Or maybe you (he, she, whoever) picked up this book, rushed right home, and opened it pronto. Or, if you're like I was once, you're standing in a bookstore right now trying to decide if this whole signing-with-baby phenomenon is worth your time — and the cost of this book. Hopefully, these ten reasons will help convince you the effort is worth both.

Reduce Frustration

I hear ya: "Great . . . where do I sign up?" But first, don't you want to know *whose* frustration is reduced? Is it yours, or is it baby's? The answer is both. Signing reduces your baby's frustration because she can communicate her needs before she's able to verbalize them with anything other than a blood-curdling scream. And signing reduces your frustration because your blood is not curdled nearly as often. Let's face it, the sooner your baby can communicate her needs in a way you can understand and respond to, the less frustrating life is for both of you.

Consider the standard wild-goose chase parents go on as baby is crying: "Is she hungry? Does something hurt? Need a change? Want up? Need help?" You know what I'm talking about, and the whole process is extremely frustrating. With signs, you get to peek into baby's mind and figure out much more quickly (and much more *quietly*) what she wants. Gotta love that.

Now I'm not saying your baby will never cry again. And I'm not saying she'll be able to communicate with signs tomorrow. I'm saying that signing is a tool you can work with to help you understand baby's world much sooner and much more clearly than you'll be able to without signs, which in turn reduces frustration all the way around.

Improve Communication Skills

Sign language is a tool your baby can use to interact with his world. He'll enjoy the fact that he can express his needs in a way you and others can understand. And you'll enjoy being able to understand him. But the communication benefits don't end there.

You've probably heard or read that most communication is nonverbal. Well, consider that with sign language, your baby is already learning to rely on and develop means other than his voice to express himself, so he's a step ahead of the game. When he learns to speak, he'll already know that his hands, his posture, and his facial expression enhance his words. Many of the first words my children spoke were words they first learned to sign.

Strengthen Family Relationships

Think about it: Your baby is paying more attention to you (looking for a sign), and you're paying more attention to her (ditto). Also, coaching baby to sign is a process. If you want your baby to sign with you, then you have to invest your time and effort in that process and in your baby. Through signing with baby, you're letting her know that you care about her because you value what she's trying to communicate. This is true for extended family, caregivers, anyone who spends time and effort in getting to know sign language and helping to coach baby.

Speaking of extended family, know up front that your in-laws will probably think you're crazy when you tell them you're showing their grandchild sign language. Mine had to see a story about signing with babies in their local newspaper before they liked the idea.

Heck, my own dad was rolling his eyes until my daughter Darby, then 10 months old, baby-stepped her way up to his aquarium on her own and began signing FISH (see Chapter 9). Then, all of a sudden, signing was the greatest thing since sliced bread.

Reap Long-Term Benefits

This is the reason many people pick up a book like this to begin with. They want their babies to be the best at everything and want to give them an edge any way they can. Although I have reservations about this motivation, the fact that signing with baby yields long-term benefits cannot be denied.

Here's the quickie scoop about two studies that prove it:

- ✔ Linda Acredolo, PhD, and Susan Goodwin, PhD, are the authors of *Baby Signs: How to Talk with Your Baby Before Your Baby Can Talk.* This was the first book devoted to nonverbal communication between parents and babies. One of the most recent studies from these pioneers established that children who used Baby Signs as infants had a 12-point higher IQ in second grade than those who did not.

- ✔ Marilyn Daniels, Professor of Speech Communication at Pennsylvania State University, is author of the book *Dancing with Words: Signing for Hearing Children's Literacy.* Daniels's research for her book followed signing children from infancy to sixth grade. The results were staggering in many areas. One of the most exciting findings is that children with Attention Deficit Disorder (ADD) or Attention Deficit Hyperactivity Disorder (ADHD) can use American Sign Language (ASL) to better focus on the world around them. Signing with your baby doesn't guarantee that he won't be diagnosed with one of these disorders in the future. But if he is, you've already given him tools to help him overcome the challenges he'll face.

Provide Extra Fun

Believe it or not, signing with baby really is a lot of fun. Signing opens doors to a whole new world of games for you and baby to play. Just imagine how signing can help fill the time on a road trip. Sign language also adds another dimension, often babies' favorite one, to story time and singing.

ASL is an incredibly expressive language, and babies are naturally drawn to and often easily amused by expressiveness. Sometimes the more dramatic you make a sign, the more baby will love it and want to make the sign, too.

Gain More Priceless Moments

As you're already aware, parenthood is filled with priceless moments. Whether they're milestones (like watching her roll over, say her first word, get her first tooth, crawl, or take those first steps) or simple things (like watching her sleep on your chest, inhaling the scent of her head, or feeling her grasp your finger in her tiny hand), these moments are some of life's true miracles. Signing adds even more.

For example, my 3-year-old daughter, Aidan Elizabeth, will from time to time catch my eye from across the room. Without a word from her or any prompting from me, she'll smile and sign I LOVE YOU (see Chapter 4). Moments like this take my breath away and make me even more thankful that I chose to sign with my children.

Develop SPI (Silent Parental Influence)

If you haven't already, you'll soon develop The Look. It's different for every parent, but it means the same thing to all children: "I'm in trouble, or I'm about to be."

Imagine supplementing and enhancing The Look with the ability to silently communicate specific words and phrases. Picture this, for example: You're at an indoor playground (you know, the kind where your kids have to remove their shoes to play), it's time to go, you catch your child's glance, and you sign, "You're FINISHED PLAYING. Get your SHOES." And he does it. Leave the yelling to the non-signing parents. (By the way, you can turn to Chapter 5 for FIN-ISHED, Chapter 10 for PLAYING, and Chapter 8 for SHOES.)

Signs are often so intuitive that this tactic sometimes even works with older, non-signing children. I volunteer at our church, and a couple of years ago I was working with a group of fifth-graders and the kids were supposed to be listening to another adult's presenta-tion. But one of my students, Caleb, was wandering around the room for a reason known only to him. I caught his eye and emphatically signed and mouthed "SIT down NOW!" He did. Later I expressed my excitement that he knew ASL. He said he didn't know ASL, but he got the message anyway. Ah, the power of signs.

Develop PSI (Parental Self Improvement)

So, when's the last time you studied another language? Granted, signing with your baby won't necessarily teach you all of ASL. However, it can give you a good foundation for the language, and you can take it as far as you choose. If you get proficient with the ASL alphabet (see Appendix A), you can finger-spell anything. In what other language can you figure out just the alphabet and then be able to communicate clearly (albeit slowly)?

Own the Spotlight

Yes, I'll admit that signing with your baby is a party trick of sorts. Complete strangers will notice you and your baby signing, and they'll stop to ask questions. Family and friends will request on-demand performances. You and your baby will be stars, owning the spotlight.

My 18-month-old, Cole, held court the other day with a group of teenagers for a good 20 minutes, as they repeatedly asked, "What else can he sign?" I told them he had a vocabulary of over 100 signs, but they wanted to see for themselves. Luckily, he had just napped and was accommodating. But if he hadn't, maybe he would've signed TIRED (see Chapter 7)!

You Never Know Where It'll Lead

My husband and I started signing with our first daughter four years ago because we thought it sounded interesting and wanted to see whether it worked. Plus, we were first-time parents and determined (some might call it neurotic) to try anything baby-related. Oh, and we lived out in the country — really, our next-door neighbors were cows — and we were looking for ways to fill our time. This is also why we ended up with our second child, born only 13½ months after her older sister. But I digress.

Eventually I became an instructor, teaching other parents how to sign with their babies. I've spoken at national conferences to groups of preschool teachers about signing in the classroom. I've led seminars for parents and play classes for caregivers and children. I've also had the privilege of working with special-needs children and their families. And now you're reading my book. I always wanted to be an author, but I never dreamed I'd be writing about signing with babies.

Signing with babies has become one of my life's passions. Who knows what doors signing with your baby will open for you?

Chapter 15

Ten Signs Every Baby and Toddler Should Know

. . . .

In This Chapter

▶ Helping your baby communicate with you

▶ Signing favorites for babies and toddlers

▶ Finding ten signs to teach your baby, even if you don't teach her any others

. . . .

*I*f you're reading this chapter, then that means either

(a) You've read everything you care to read elsewhere in this book, and now you want to confirm which ten signs to definitely use with your baby.

or

(b) You're ready to jump in with both feet, and you don't currently have time to read the details that go along with these signs elsewhere in this book.

So for your easy reference — or your need for speed — this chapter provides the bare-bones directions for ten of the most important and useful signs for babies and toddlers.

Bed

Follow these steps (and check out Chapter 7 for details about this sign and others related to it):

1. **Place the palm of your hand on your ear.**

2. **Tilt your head to the same side as if you're using your hand for a pillow (see Figure 15-1).**

Figure 15-1: BED.

Eat

Follow these steps (and check out Chapter 5 for details about this sign and others related to it):

1. **Make a flat-O hand shape by first forming an *O* with your fingers and thumb and then flattening them out so that it looks like a deflated balloon (see Chapter 3).**

2. **Touch your fingertips to your mouth repeatedly (see Figure 15-2).**

Figure 15-2: EAT.

Finished

Follow these steps (and check out Chapter 5 for details about this sign and others related to it):

1. **Place both hands in the air, near your shoulders, finger-tips pointing up, palms facing away from your body.**

2. **Rotate your hands at the wrists so that your palms face your body.**

3. **Repeat the rotation several times (see Figure 15-3).**

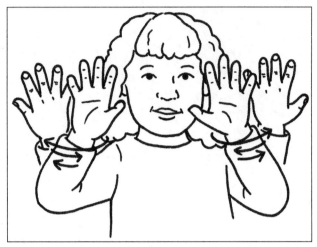

Figure 15-3: FINISHED.

Help

Follow these steps (and check out Chapter 6 for details about this sign and others related to it):

1. **Place a fist, thumb up, on top of the opposite palm.**

2. **While keeping that position, move both hands up (see Figure 15-4).**

Figure 15-4: HELP.

Hurt

Follow these steps (and check out Chapter 6 for details about this sign and others related to it):

1. **Extend both index fingers and repeatedly almost touch their tips.**

   That action signs HURT in general. If you want to show a specific place on the body that HURTS, read Step 2. If you want to show that feelings are HURT, skip Step 2 and read Step 3.

2. **If a specific body part HURTS, move your hands to the vicinity of the body part that hurts while doing Step 1.**

3. **If feelings are HURT instead of a body part, twist your hands and fingers in opposite directions over your heart while doing Step 1 and making a sad face (see Figure 15-5).**

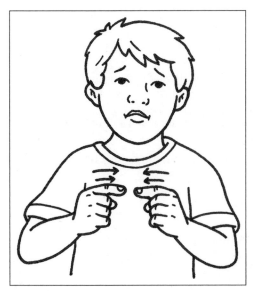

Figure 15-5: HURT.

Milk

Follow these steps (and check out Chapter 5 for details about this sign and others related to it):

1. **Imagine that a cow is standing right beside you.**

2. **Open and close the fist of one hand several times, little finger closest to the floor (see Figure 15-6).**

Figure 15-6: MILK.

More

Follow these steps (and check out Chapter 5 for details about this sign and others related to it):

1. **Using both hands, make two flat-O hand shapes (see Chapter 3).**

2. **Repeatedly touch the fingertips of both hands (see Figure 15-7).**

Figure 15-7: MORE.

Please

Follow these steps:

1. **Place your palm flat against your chest like you're about to say the Pledge of Allegiance.**

2. **Make a circle with your palm on your chest with a quizzical look on your face (see Figure 15-8).**

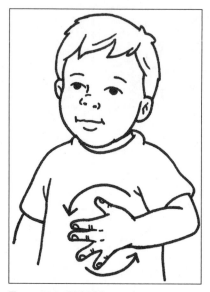

Figure 15-8: PLEASE.

Stop

Follow these steps (and check out Chapter 6 for details about this sign and others related to it):

1. **Hold out one hand as if preparing to shake hands with someone.**

2. **Hold out your opposite hand so that the palm is facing up.**

3. **Use the edge of Step 1's hand to come down sharply on your opposite hand's palm (see Figure 15-9).**

Figure 15-9: STOP.

Thank You

Follow these steps (and check out Chapter 4 for details about this sign and others related to it):

1. **Place the tips of your fingers on your chin.**

2. **In one gesture, move your hand down with your finger-tips pointing away from your chin (see Figure 15-10).**

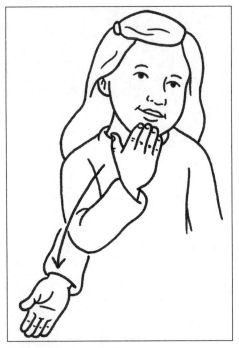

Figure 15-10: THANK YOU.

Chapter 16

Ten (Or So) Songs to Sign

*S*igning and singing with children go together as naturally as peas and carrots. In fact, lots of children's songs already have motions to them, but be careful to be clear that they're "motions" and not actual signs. That's how our family has dealt with our girls coming home from preschool and saying, "Look, I learned the signs for a song!" My husband and I always explain (over and over and over again) that they've learned the *motions* to the song, and then we show them what the actual signs for the words look like. Granted, as a result, my firstborn, Darby, who's 4, has been known to tell her teachers that she's not learning signs today; she's just learning motions and her mommy will teach her the signs when she gets home from school. A little embarrassing, yes, but at least she knows what she's talking about.

Anyway, this chapter gets you started with ten (minus two, but let's face it, only a pooterhead would actually count and then tattletale to my publisher) well-known children's songs to sign. Note that I haven't included each and every verse of these songs — just the main verse or two that most children become very familiar with. I hope you and baby enjoy this experience.

 I highly recommend that you pick out one or two words to sign from each song instead of trying to sign all the words. Pick words that occur frequently in the song or are part of the climax of the song so that you can be dramatic and call attention to those particular signs. And don't forget to have fun!

The Itsy Bitsy Spider

When I'm talking to people about signing with babies or toddlers, I like to point out the differences between signing "The Itsy Bitsy Spider" and doing the motions we're all familiar with. For this song, I recommend that at first you pick out just one or two of the following signs to use with baby: WATER (see Chapter 7), RAIN (see Chapter 10), SUN (see Chapter 10), and SPIDER, which isn't covered elsewhere in this book so here are the directions:

1. **Make claw-C hand shapes with both hands (see Chapter 3), palms facing down.**

2. **Cross one hand over the other.**

3. **Wiggle your fingers like the legs of a spider (see Figure 16-1).**

Figure 16-1: Itsy Bitsy SPIDER.

After you choose the one or two signs you're going to focus on with baby, sing and sign away:

The itsy bitsy SPIDER

Climbed up the WATER spout.

Down came the RAIN

And washed the SPIDER out.

Out came the SUN

And dried up all the RAIN.

And the itsy bitsy SPIDER

Climbed up the spout again.

Old MacDonald

A favorite among children of all ages, this song is a great way to practice the various animal signs found in Chapter 9. The following example uses DUCK, but Chapter 9 also covers the signs for COW, HORSE, SHEEP, PIG, CHICKEN, and FROG, as well as various pets and zoo animals:

Old MacDonald had a farm

e-i-e-i-o

On this farm he had a DUCK

e-i-e-i-o

With a quack quack here [sign DUCK as you say "quack"]

And a quack quack there

Here a quack, there a quack

Everywhere a quack quack

Old MacDonald had a farm

e-i-e-i-o

Row, Row, Row Your Boat

This song is a favorite at bath time or when my children visit their grandparents' lake house. Two signs are great to use while singing this song: BOAT, which you can find in Chapter 10, and HAPPY (used for *merrily*), which you can find in Chapter 6. Here you go:

Row, row, row your BOAT

Gently down the stream

Merrily, merrily, merrily, merrily [sign HAPPY as you sing "merrily"]

Life is but a dream.

Twinkle, Twinkle Little Star

When my oldest child, Darby, was a toddler, she sang and signed this song to every baby she came across, after getting tons of practice singing and signing it to her baby sister, Aidan Elizabeth. I've actually seen Darby stop a crying baby in a crowded store by working her magic with this song. And Aidan Elizabeth could carry this tune while signing it long before she could sing the words to it. So, yes, it's absolutely a Watson family favorite. Hopefully, it'll be a favorite of your family's, too.

As for which signs to use, I recommend that at first you choose among STAR (Chapter 10), WHAT (Chapter 1), and UP, which isn't covered elsewhere in this book but is a breeze to make: Just point to the sky, and you've signed UP.

Now that you have your signs, here's your song:

Twinkle, twinkle little STAR

How I wonder WHAT you are

UP above the world so high

Like a diamond in the sky

Twinkle, twinkle little STAR

How I wonder WHAT you are

Baa, Baa Black Sheep

This song is a fun way to help children understand that wool comes from sheep. In fact, the sign for SHEEP mimics shearing a sheep (see Chapter 9). In addition, you can substitute other colors for *black* in the song, giving you an opportunity to practice some color signs (various ones, including BLACK, are covered in Appendix C). And if you'd like to sign the word YES in the song (just because it's fun), form the sign by making an ASL letter *S* (see Appendix A) and simply pretending it's a head nodding "yes." Got it? Good! Here you go:

Baa, baa BLACK SHEEP

Have you any wool?

YES sir, YES sir

Three bags full

One for my master

One for my dame

One for the little boy

Who lives in the lane

Baa, baa BLACK SHEEP

Have you any wool?

YES sir, YES sir

Three bags full

Mary Had a Little Lamb

This song is always a hit with babies and toddlers. And if you want, you can make substitutions in this song, too. For example, you can substitute your child's name for *Mary* and substitute other animals for *lamb* to practice various animal signs (see Chapter 9). And feel free to substitute other colors for *white* to practice color signs (see Appendix C). Note that the sign for LAMB is the same as SHEEP (see Chapter 9) and the sign for SNOW is in Chapter 10. With that info in your back pocket, you're good to go:

Mary had a little LAMB

Little LAMB, little LAMB

Mary had a little LAMB

Its fleece was WHITE as SNOW

The Alphabet Song

If you're not singing the ABC song yet, you will be soon. Learning the alphabet is an important part of childhood and the foundation for learning to read and write. I've lost count of the number of times we sing this song daily in our house.

The signs for the alphabet are in Appendix A, but obviously you won't expect a baby or toddler to make all these signs. Signing these individual letters will likely be fun down the road, at around school age:

A, B, C, D, E, F, G,

H, I, J, K, L, M, N, O, P,

Q, R, S,

T, U, V,

W, X, Y, and Z

Now I know my ABCs

Tell me what you think of me.

I've Been Working on the Railroad

My son Cole's fascination with trains began early and continues to grow on a daily basis. Cole likes for everyone in my family to sing this song for him so he can sign TRAIN (see Chapter 10) and make the train-whistle sound. Besides using the sign for TRAIN in this song, you and your baby can also use the sign for WORK, which you make like so:

1. **Make two fists, palms down, and place one fist on top of the other.**

2. **Hit the bottom fist with the top one a few times (see Figure 16-2).**

Figure 16-2: WORKing hard.

Now put those signs to good use:

I've been WORKing on the RAILROAD [sign TRAIN]

All the livelong day

I've been WORKing on the RAILROAD

Just to pass the time away.

Can't you hear the whistle blowing? [make a whistle sound]

Rise up so early in the morn?

Can't you hear the captain shouting,

"Dinah, blow your horn?"

Chapter 17

Ten (Or So) Signing Resources

In This Chapter

▶ Visiting Web sites to get help with baby signing

▶ Finding DVDs to assist you in signing with your baby

▶ Finding classes and other resources for more signing info

*E*ven if I wanted to, I couldn't get every little detail about sign-ing with your baby in this book. My goal, of course, is just to cover the basics, but know that there's a lot more info out there. If you decide that you want to tap into it, you may want to start with one or more of the ten resources listed in this chapter. These resources will assist you in finding more ways to sign with your baby, as well as finding signs not covered in this book.

ASLPro.com

This site (www.aslpro.com), which serves as a reference and offers learning tools, gives you access to thousands of American Sign Language (ASL) signs. It even includes a specific section of signs that can be difficult to find elsewhere.

ImaginationSigners.com

This is my personal Web site, so of course, it's the best one. You can find it at www.imaginationsigners.com. At this site, you can purchase some of these recommended signing products and check out my class and seminar schedules, as well as contact me with news on how signing is going for you and yours.

Little Signers, Inc.

This site (www.littlesigners.com) is run by a group of ASL inter-preters who teach classes, offer lots of pointers, and sell ASL books that are not always easily found elsewhere.

Sign2Me.com

This site (www.sign2me.com) is the Web site of Joseph Garcia, one of the pioneers in the area of signing with babies. This site is a great resource for info about signing with babies. In addition, it offers signing classes based on the research of Joseph Garcia, a pioneer in the field of baby signing and an advocate of ASL instead of invented gestures.

Signing with Your Baby

A mom who loves signing with children put together this amazing and comprehensive Web site (www.signingbaby.com) on signing with babies. The site includes tips, forums, and an online store.

Baby Einstein's Baby Wordsworth First Words — Around the House

With a famous face or two, this Baby Einstein DVD is big fun on the signing spectrum. Look for about 45 signs within its 45 minutes. Lots of fun signs are here, including the sign for computer. You can go to www.babyeinstein.com and, in the Product Search box at the top of the page, type **Baby Wordsworth** and then click the Search button. You'll be taken to a page where you can find this DVD, among other products.

Signing Smart

At www.signingsmart.com, you can find info on the research done by the founders of the Signing Smart program, Dr. Michele Anthony and Dr. Reyna Lindert. Signing Smart offers play classes and parent workshops, and the program focuses on strategies to make signing with your baby more productive. It's a very comprehensive curriculum and is even offered internationally. All signs are ASL signs.

Developed to go with Signing Smart's handbooks and book, the *Signing Smart Treasure Chest,* Volume 1 and Volume 2, videos encompass Signing Smart strategies and signs featured in Signing Smart's books and classes. Approximate running time is 30 minutes per volume. You can order them through www.signingsmart.com. From the home page, click on Store, and you'll find all kinds of resources.

Kindermusik has teamed up with Signing Smart to create a music and signing class. Sing and Sign is an eight-week course and is taught by Kindermusik instructors found globally. All signs are ASL signs. You can find more about these classes at the Kindermusik Web site (www.kindermusik.com).

Signing Time

Oh, the number of children I have seen discover ASL from the video series offered through this site. Personally, I've used these videos with kids in all grades of elementary school, as well as with my own kids. In the videos, Alex, who is a hearing child, and Leah, who is deaf, along with Leah's mom, Rachel, will sign, sing, and dance their way into your heart. There are 13 volumes in the *Signing Time* series and two volumes focusing on babies as well. *Signing Time* sells books and flashcards, too. *Signing Time* may even be on your local PBS station. All signs are ASL signs. At www.signingtime.com you can find loads of resources to help teach hearing children, deaf children, and special-needs children how to use ASL.

The first time my 2-year-old signing baby Darby watched a *Signing Time* DVD, she picked up three signs. When I started watching *Signing Time* DVDs with my kids two years ago, there were only three volumes. Obviously, with 13 DVDs now available, the company's sales have exploded. You'll see why when you see them. For a sneak peak, you can check out your local PBS station and see if *Signing Time* is broadcast there. The DVDs and the show are approximately 30 minutes each. And you can find out more about ordering them by going to www.signingtime.com/products/.

Tiny Fingers

Tiny Fingers (www.tinyfingers.com) offers classes in
Washington, D.C., Maryland, and Virginia. The classes have been
developed and are taught by a certified ASL interpreter. All signs
are ASL signs.

Baby Fingers

Baby Fingers (www.mybabyfingers.com) offers classes throughout
New York City. Class options are available for very young infants
through preschool-aged children. All signs are ASL signs.

Baby Signs

Dr. Linda Acredolo and Dr. Susan Goodwyn provided the initial
research on signing with hearing babies. Through the Baby Signs
site (www.babysigns.com), they offer classes in baby signing internationally. Their *Baby Signs* curriculum and book are ASL-based,
but they also advocate invented gestures.

Gymboree's Sign & Play classes are offered through a cooperative
effort between Gymboree (www.gymboree.com) and Baby Signs.
The classes, which span six weeks, cover signs to incorporate into
daily life.

KiddiesSigns.com

This site (www.kiddiessigns.com) is awesome. You can rent and
buy software or DVDs of signing kids in several situations. There
are options for songs, stories, and the ASL alphabet. One unique
feature of this series is that you can choose the ethnic background
of the child in your rental or purchase. Another unique and amazing feature is that this series actually teaches ASL in full, not just
the individual signs for certain objects, so hearing-impaired people
and their families can benefit from it, too.

HandSpeak

For a small fee, you can access the wealth of information on ASL
that the HandSpeak Web site offers (www.handspeak.com). This

site has a section on signing with baby, and it focuses on signs pertinent to *life* with baby — always a good thing.

Baby Hands Productions

The Web site of Baby Hands Productions (www.mybabycantalk.com) offers a DVD series that's best described by the site itself: "These DVDs are the first baby sign language learning programs that feature preverbal babies signing all of the words presented. Babies love to watch this video and they learn to sign!" All signs are ASL signs.

Part VI
Appendixes

The 5th Wave   By Rich Tennant

"I always sign to the kids in a quiet and respectful way, but occasionally I wear this to add a little punctuation."

In this part . . .

My husband lost his appendix when he was 10 years old. I was able to hold on to mine until just a couple of years ago. So there are only three appendixes left in my home (unless fish have them, too). In honor of my three appendix-laden children, in this book I include three appendixes (my husband says "appendices" . . . oh well, tomāto/tomäto).

Letters, numbers, colors — they're all a part of growing up, whether you sign with your children or not. You can enhance their experience when they get there by adding signs for, say, the ABCs, the numbers one through ten, and some common colors, which are the focus of Part VI. Note too that various alphabet and number signs are often used as starting points to create other signs. You can see this principle applied in Appendix C, as the signs for most common colors begin with a letter sign. And, trust me, baby will *love* signing his favorite colors. So add these three sets of signs to your signing vocabulary, and your baby will reap the rewards.

Appendix A

The ASL Alphabet

A h, the ABC song. If you're a parent of a baby or toddler, know that you'll eventually sing that song 'til you're blue in the face, and then some. Even though the alphabet is probably not a major deal right now, it will become pretty important to both you and your sweet baby. It's the foundation of that ever-important primary goal of elementary school: learning to read.

In the meantime, the American Sign Language (ASL) alphabet (shown in Figures A-1 through A-26) can become pretty important to you and your baby. Many ASL word signs begin with a specific ASL letter sign, so knowing the ASL alphabet can give you a jump-start on some word signs. The bonus is that when your little bundle of joy eventually goes off for his first year of school and learning the alphabet becomes more important, the ASL alphabet will provide a fun way for you and your budding student to practice the alphabet together. Plus, if you know the ASL alphabet, you can fingerspell any word in the English language. Have fun!

Figure A-1: A.

Figure A-2: B.

Figure A-3: C.

Figure A-4: D.

Figure A-5: E.

Figure A-6: F.

Figure A-7: G.

Figure A-8: H.

Figure A-9: I.

Figure A-10: J.

Figure A-11: K.

Figure A-12: L.

Figure A-13: M.

Figure A-14: N.

Figure A-15: O.

Figure A-16: P.

Figure A-17: Q.

Figure A-18: R.

Figure A-19: S.

Figure A-20: T.

Figure A-21: U.

Figure A-22: V.

Figure A-23: W.

Figure A-24: X.

Figure A-25: Y.

Figure A-26: Z.

Appendix B

ASL Numbers

● ●

*A*merican Sign Language (ASL) numbers aren't used much when you're signing with babies and toddlers. However, out of curiosity, lots of people always ask me to show them some specific ASL number signs. So, just to pacify your curiosity, here are the numbers one through ten, ASL-style (see Figures B-1 through B-10). Happy counting!

Figure B-1: One.

Figure B-2: Two.

Figure B-3: Three.

Figure B-4: Four.

Figure B-5: Five.

Figure B-6: Six.

Figure B-7: Seven.

Figure B-8: Eight.

Figure B-9: Nine.

Figure B-10: Ten.

Appendix C

ASL Colors

● ●

*C*olors are a vital part of children's lives. Colors identify children's preferences — their very *strong* preferences. For example, Sally only wears the green shirt, and Sarah only wears the pink one. Or the blue bike is Bobby's, and the red one is Billy's. Or the only color food that Margie will eat is orange because it's her favorite color, which requires you to explain to the pediatrician and sundry nosy Nellies why her skin is tinged a bit orange, but aren't you glad she's at least eating some veggies thrown in with those orange cheesy chips?

A great game for you to play when she gets older is "I spy. . . ." Finish the sentence by saying and signing a color (and eventually just signing a color to exercise her memory banks). In the meantime, start by showing your baby or toddler her favorite colors with signs. This appendix provides some basic colors to choose from.

Red

To sign RED, think about brushing the color on your lips:

Using the tip of your index finger, brush your lips two times.

You're making an ASL number ONE (see Appendix B) hand shape as you brush your lips, and bringing it to an ASL letter *X* (see Appendix A), as shown in Figure C-1.

Figure C-1: Red.

Pink

The sign for PINK uses the same hand movement as the sign for RED (see the preceding section), except you use a different finger:

1. **Make the sign for the ASL letter *P* (see Appendix A).**

2. **While holding that position, brush your middle finger against your lips two times (see Figure C-2).**

Figure C-2: Pink.

Orange

To sign ORANGE, pretend you're squeezing the juice of an orange into your mouth:

1. **Make a claw-C hand shape (see Chapter 3) in front of your lower face, thumb facing your mouth.**

2. **Close the claw-C hand shape into an ASL letter *S* (see Appendix A) two times, as shown in Figure C-3.**

Figure C-3: Orange.

Yellow

Whether you're singing about a yellow submarine or I Spying a yellow banana peeking out of the fruit bowl, here's how to two-step the sign for YELLOW all the while:

1. **Make an ASL letter *Y* (see Appendix A), palm facing away from your body.**

2. **While holding that position, twist your hand at your wrist a few times (see Figure C-4).**

Figure C-4: Yellow.

Green

The color of money. The color of spring. The color of Kermit and of emerald bling. Here's how to sign GREEN:

1. **Make an ASL letter *G* (see Appendix A), finger pointing away from you.**

2. **While holding that position, twist your hand at your wrist a few times (see Figure C-5).**

Figure C-5: Green.

Blue

Whether your sweetie loves blue because it's the color of the bright, clear sky or because she has blue eyes or because her very first stuffed animal was blue, here's how to show her the sign:

1. **Make an ASL letter *B* (see Appendix A), palm facing away from you.**

2. **While holding that position, twist your hand at your wrist a few times (see Figure C-6).**

Figure C-6: Blue.

Purple

Purple mountain majesties, purple dinosaurs, purple oopsy bruises, purple grape-juiced lips. I can think of plenty of occasions to sign PURPLE:

1. **Make an ASL letter *P* (see Appendix A).**

2. **While holding that position, twist your hand back and forth a few times (see Figure C-7).**

Figure C-7: Purple.

Brown

Go figure. To sign BROWN, you need to pretend you're tracing a sideburn on your cheek:

1. **Make an ASL letter *B* (see Appendix A), palm facing out with your thumb touching your temple.**

2. **While holding that position, slide your thumb down the side of your face until your thumb is touching your jaw (see Figure C-8).**

Figure C-8: Brown.

Black

Signing BLACK is so easy that step-by-step directions aren't necessary. Just slide your index finger above both eyebrows (see Figure C-9). That's it. Well, maybe add in thoughts of a unibrow just for kicks.

Figure C-9: Black.

White

When there's a baby or toddler in the house, white things don't tend to stay white for very long. But that's beside the point, which is simply how to sign (even not-so-bright) WHITE:

1. **Place your hand flat in the middle of your chest.**

2. **Pull your hand away from you into a flat-O hand shape (see Chapter 3), as shown in Figure C-10.**

Figure C-10: White.

Colors

Sometimes you'll want to communicate about colors in general instead of talking and signing about one particular color. No problem.

When you make this sign, think of your individual fingers as various different colors.

1. Make an open-5 hand shape (see Chapter 3), palm facing you.
2. Wiggle your fingers at your chin (see Figure C-11).

Figure C-11: Colors.

Rainbow

Rainbows are prominent in children's décor, bedding, storybooks, and coloring books. And seeing a real rainbow for the very first time is quite a special moment. Be on the lookout for opportunities to sign this beautiful phenomenon:

1. Make the sign for COLORS (see the preceding section).
2. Keeping an open-5 hand shape (see Chapter 3), turn your palm facing out and draw an arc in the air to represent a rainbow (see Figure C-12).

Figure C-12: Rainbow.

Now go forth and color your world. Watch out! Baby may color the walls instead.

Index

• *G* •

• *Q* •

Notes

Notes

Notes

Notes

Notes

Notes

Notes

BUSINESS, CAREERS & PERSONAL FINANCE

0-7645-5307-0   0-7645-5331-3 *†

Also available:

- Accounting For Dummies †
  0-7645-5314-3
- Business Plans Kit For Dummies †
  0-7645-5365-8
- Cover Letters For Dummies
  0-7645-5224-4
- Frugal Living For Dummies
  0-7645-5403-4
- Leadership For Dummies
  0-7645-5176-0
- Managing For Dummies
  0-7645-1771-6

- Marketing For Dummies
  0-7645-5600-2
- Personal Finance For Dummies *
  0-7645-2590-5
- Project Management
  For Dummies
  0-7645-5283-X
- Resumes For Dummies †
  0-7645-5471-9
- Selling For Dummies
  0-7645-5363-1
- Small Business Kit For Dummies *†
  0-7645-5093-4

HOME & BUSINESS COMPUTER BASICS

0-7645-4074-2   0-7645-3758-X

Also available:

- ACT! 6 For Dummies
  0-7645-2645-6
- iLife '04 All-in-One Desk Reference
  For Dummies
  0-7645-7347-0
- iPAQ For Dummies
  0-7645-6769-1
- Mac OS X Panther Timesaving
  Techniques For Dummies
  0-7645-5812-9
- Macs For Dummies
  0-7645-5656-8
- Microsoft Money 2004 For Dummies
  0-7645-4195-1

- Office 2003 All-in-One Desk
  Reference For Dummies
  0-7645-3883-7
- Outlook 2003 For Dummies
  0-7645-3759-8
- PCs For Dummies
  0-7645-4074-2
- TiVo For Dummies
  0-7645-6923-6
- Upgrading and Fixing PCs
  For Dummies
  0-7645-1665-5
- Windows XP Timesaving
  Techniques For Dummies
  0-7645-3748-2

FOOD, HOME, GARDEN, HOBBIES, MUSIC & PETS

0-7645-5295-3   0-7645-5232-5

Also available:

- Bass Guitar For Dummies
  0-7645-2487-9
- Diabetes Cookbook For Dummies
  0-7645-5230-9
- Gardening For Dummies *
  0-7645-5130-2
- Guitar For Dummies
  0-7645-5106-X
- Holiday Decorating For Dummies
  0-7645-2570-0
- Home Improvement All-in-One
  For Dummies
  0-7645-5680-0

- Knitting For Dummies
  0-7645-5395-X
- Piano For Dummies
  0-7645-5105-1
- Puppies For Dummies
  0-7645-5255-4
- Scrapbooking For Dummies
  0-7645-7208-3
- Senior Dogs For Dummies
  0-7645-5818-8
- Singing For Dummies
  0-7645-2475-5
- 30-Minute Meals For Dummies
  0-7645-2589-1

INTERNET & DIGITAL MEDIA

0-7645-1664-7   0-7645-6924-4

Also available:

- 2005 Online Shopping Directory
  For Dummies
  0-7645-7495-7
- CD & DVD Recording For Dummies
  0-7645-5956-7
- eBay For Dummies
  0-7645-5654-1
- Fighting Spam For Dummies
  0-7645-5965-6
- Genealogy Online For Dummies
  0-7645-5964-8
- Google For Dummies
  0-7645-4420-9

- Home Recording For Musicians
  For Dummies
  0-7645-1634-5
- The Internet For Dummies
  0-7645-4173-0
- iPod & iTunes For Dummies
  0-7645-7772-7
- Preventing Identity Theft
  For Dummies
  0-7645-7336-5
- Pro Tools All-in-One Desk
  Reference For Dummies
  0-7645-5714-9
- Roxio Easy Media Creator
  For Dummies
  0-7645-7131-1

* Separate Canadian edition also available

† Separate U.K. edition also available

Available wherever books are sold. For more information or to order direct: U.S. customers visit www.dummies.com or call 1-877-762-2974.
U.K. customers visit www.wileyeurope.com or call 0800 243407. Canadian customers visit www.wiley.ca or call 1-800-567-4797.

SPORTS, FITNESS, PARENTING, RELIGION & SPIRITUALITY

0-7645-5146-9   0-7645-5418-2

Also available:

Adoption For Dummies
0-7645-5488-3

Basketball For Dummies
0-7645-5248-1

The Bible For Dummies
0-7645-5296-1

Buddhism For Dummies
0-7645-5359-3

Catholicism For Dummies
0-7645-5391-7

Hockey For Dummies
0-7645-5228-7

Judaism For Dummies
0-7645-5299-6

Martial Arts For Dummies
0-7645-5358-5

Pilates For Dummies
0-7645-5397-6

Religion For Dummies
0-7645-5264-3

Teaching Kids to Read
For Dummies
0-7645-4043-2

Weight Training For Dummies
0-7645-5168-X

Yoga For Dummies
0-7645-5117-5

TRAVEL

0-7645-5438-7   0-7645-5453-0

Also available:

Alaska For Dummies
0-7645-1761-9

Arizona For Dummies
0-7645-6938-4

Cancún and the Yucatán
For Dummies
0-7645-2437-2

Cruise Vacations For Dummies
0-7645-6941-4

Europe For Dummies
0-7645-5456-5

Ireland For Dummies
0-7645-5455-7

Las Vegas For Dummies
0-7645-5448-4

London For Dummies
0-7645-4277-X

New York City For Dummies
0-7645-6945-7

Paris For Dummies
0-7645-5494-8

RV Vacations For Dummies
0-7645-5443-3

Walt Disney World & Orlando
For Dummies
0-7645-6943-0

GRAPHICS, DESIGN & WEB DEVELOPMENT

0-7645-4345-8   0-7645-5589-8

Also available:

Adobe Acrobat 6 PDF
For Dummies
0-7645-3760-1

Building a Web Site For Dummies
0-7645-7144-3

Dreamweaver MX 2004
For Dummies
0-7645-4342-3

FrontPage 2003 For Dummies
0-7645-3882-9

HTML 4 For Dummies
0-7645-1995-6

Illustrator CS For Dummies
0-7645-4084-X

Macromedia Flash MX 2004
For Dummies
0-7645-4358-X

Photoshop 7 All-in-One Desk
Reference For Dummies
0-7645-1667-1

Photoshop CS Timesaving
Techniques For Dummies
0-7645-6782-9

PHP 5 For Dummies
0-7645-4166-8

PowerPoint 2003 For Dummies
0-7645-3908-6

QuarkXPress 6 For Dummies
0-7645-2593-X

NETWORKING, SECURITY, PROGRAMMING & DATABASES

0-7645-6852-3   0-7645-5784-X

Also available:

A+ Certification For Dummies
0-7645-4187-0

Access 2003 All-in-One Desk
Reference For Dummies
0-7645-3988-4

Beginning Programming
For Dummies
0-7645-4997-9

C For Dummies
0-7645-7068-4

Firewalls For Dummies
0-7645-4048-3

Home Networking For Dummies
0-7645-42796

Network Security For Dummies
0-7645-1679-5

Networking For Dummies
0-7645-1677-9

TCP/IP For Dummies
0-7645-1760-0

VBA For Dummies
0-7645-3989-2

Wireless All In-One Desk Reference
For Dummies
0-7645-7496-5

Wireless Home Networking
For Dummies
0-7645-3910-8

HEALTH & SELF-HELP

0-7645-6820-5 *†   0-7645-2566-2

Also available:

Alzheimer's For Dummies
0-7645-3899-3

Asthma For Dummies
0-7645-4233-8

Controlling Cholesterol For Dummies
0-7645-5440-9

Depression For Dummies
0-7645-3900-0

Dieting For Dummies
0-7645-4149-8

Fertility For Dummies
0-7645-2549-2

Fibromyalgia For Dummies
0-7645-5441-7

Improving Your Memory For Dummies
0-7645-5435-2

Pregnancy For Dummies †
0-7645-4483-7

Quitting Smoking For Dummies
0-7645-2629-4

Relationships For Dummies
0-7645-5384-4

Thyroid For Dummies
0-7645-5385-2

EDUCATION, HISTORY, REFERENCE & TEST PREPARATION

0-7645-5194-9   0-7645-4186-2

Also available:

Algebra For Dummies
0-7645-5325-9

British History For Dummies
0-7645-7021-8

Calculus For Dummies
0-7645-2498-4

English Grammar For Dummies
0-7645-5322-4

Forensics For Dummies
0-7645-5580-4

The GMAT For Dummies
0-7645-5251-1

Inglés Para Dummies
0-7645-5427-1

Italian For Dummies
0-7645-5196-5

Latin For Dummies
0-7645-5431-X

Lewis & Clark For Dummies
0-7645-2545-X

Research Papers For Dummies
0-7645-5426-3

The SAT I For Dummies
0-7645-7193-1

Science Fair Projects For Dummies
0-7645-5460-3

U.S. History For Dummies
0-7645-5249-X

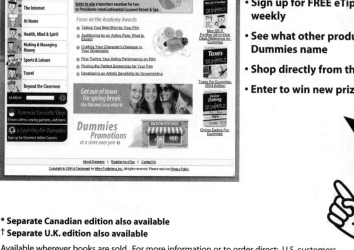

Get smart @ dummies.com®

- **Find a full list of Dummies titles**
- **Look into loads of FREE on-site articles**
- **Sign up for FREE eTips e-mailed to you weekly**
- **See what other products carry the Dummies name**
- **Shop directly from the Dummies bookstore**
- **Enter to win new prizes every month!**

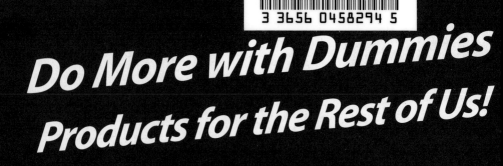